BEYOND THE DAMS
TO THE TIRPITZ

ALAN W. COOPER

617 Squadron of RAF Bomber Command became a legend in 1943 when a force of Avro Lancasters breached the Möhne and Eder Dams in Germany. The Lancasters were flown by hand-picked crews, chosen for their proven ability and skill in bomber operations. Yet the Dams Raid was only one raid, the first of nearly 100 undertaken by the Squadron.

In the main they were special targets, needing special treatment and the determination of the special crews to destroy them. The targets were hard nuts to crack: viaducts, solid U-Boat pens, V-weapon sites, German battleships, aircraft factories, etc. All needed to be illuminated, marked and bombed, often at low level, and using huge bombs of 12,000 lb or later 22,000 lb. The men who took these bombs to these targets were a special breed, their courage and skill paramount.

Wing Commander Guy Gibson VC, DSO & bar, DFC & bar, formed the Squadron. His successors were men like George Holden DSO DFC, Leonard Cheshire VC DSO and two bars DFC, Willie Tait DSO and three bars, DFC and bar, Johnny Fauquier DSO and two bars DFC. The men under them had to live up to their impressive records.

By the end of World War Two the Squadron's name had become more than just a legend; the 'Dam Busters' were a part of history and an élite within the ranks of Bomber Command.

By the same author

The Men Who Breached the Dams (1982)
Bombers Over Berlin (1985)
In Action with the Enemy (1986)
Free to Fight Again (1988)
Battle of the Ruhr (1991)

BEYOND THE DAMS
TO THE TIRPITZ

The Later Operations
of 617 Squadron

ALAN W. COOPER

GOODALL PUBLICATIONS LTD
London & St. Albans

Copyright © by Alan W. Cooper 1991

First published in Great Britain in 1983
by William Kimber & Co. Ltd

First Goodall Publications paperback edition 1991

Front cover: From an oil painting by Peter Coombs
Design: Peter Gunthorpe

A catalogue record for this book is available
from the British Library

GOODALL PUBLICATIONS LIMITED
London and St. Albans

Phototypesetting in 11/13 Baskerville

Reproduced, printed and bound in Great Britain by
BPCC Hazell Books, Aylesbury, Bucks, England
Member of BPCC Ltd.

ISBN 0 907579 15 9

Contents

This book is dedicated to the memory of the men of 617 Squadron who in WWII failed to return from operations, or were killed flying with the Squadron.

They gave the dearest thing any man can give, their lives. We shall not forget them.

Acknowledgements

This book is based on the records and recollections of many people, and I am grateful for their co-operation and that of many institutions. A list of their names can be found at the end of this book but in particular my thanks are due to my friend Horst Muller, John Evans and to Norman Franks for his help in the presentation of this book.

My thanks also are due to the Imperial War Museum, Public Records Office, Royal Air Force Museum, Air Historical Branch, Commonwealth War Graves, Royal Air Force Records Gloucester and Adastral House, and last but not least the staff of William Kimber & Co.

CHAPTER ONE

After the Dams

Number 617 Squadron had been formed in March 1943 specifically to train for a raid on, and then finally to attack, four dams in the Ruhr Valley. This one operation, which gave undying fame to the squadron and captured the imagination of both civilian and serviceman alike, took place on the night of 16/17 May 1943.

The details of this raid I covered in detail in my first book, *The Men who Breached the Dams*.[1] On that night a force of nineteen specially adapted four-engined Avro Lancasters, flew to Germany, lost eight of their number but smashed two of the dams, the Möhne and the Eder, and damaged the Sorpe. Fifty-three aircrew died that night while three others were taken captive.

Few other single operations flown by squadrons of Bomber Command are remembered so vividly as this one. The men and the squadron became known universally as 'The Dam Busters'. For 617 Squadron, however, the dams were to become just the first of several 'special targets' that needed 'special' treatment.

*

The squadron had been formed under the leadership of Wing Commander Guy Penrose Gibson, DSO & bar, DFC & bar. When given the task he had just completed a third tour of operations, two on bombers and one on night fighters. The Dams Raid had been his 74th bombing mission since the war began.

Following the euphoria of their successful attack, 617 Squadron were stood down from operations and Guy Gibson informed that he

[1] Published by Wm. Kimber & Co, 1982.

had done enough. The award of the Victoria Cross was his reward for his superb leadership and heroism during the raid itself. He was still only twenty-four years old and now the most highly decorated operational pilot in the Royal Air Force.

The squadron had been manned by a number of men who had just completed or had nearly completed bomber tours or recently begun second tours, plus a few who had, on average, almost a third of a tour under their belt. It was obvious that with such a nucleus of experienced men with success just behind them, 617 would not be immediately disbanded and its men returned to their former units, or go off to begin instructing at Operational Training Units. The majority stayed. However Flight Sergeant Cyril Anderson and his crew decided to return to 49 Squadron on 3rd June. They did not locate their target – the Sorpe Dam – and had flown home with their Special Bomb. They were replaced by Flying Officer W.H. Kellaway, DSO, in from 149 Squadron at the end of the month.

The survivors of the Dams Raid who stayed on with 617 were an experienced bunch, Micky Martin, at twenty-five, held the DSO and DFC and had flown a total of 36 bombing operations since late 1941, with both 455 and 50 Squadrons. David Maltby, DSO, DFC, aged twenty-three, he and his crew had completed a tour with 106 and 97 Squadrons. Les Knight, an Australian like Martin, had a DSO and a tour with 50 Squadron behind him. He was twenty-two Another Australian was Dave Shannon, whose youthful looks belied his twenty-one years of age, (he had been only twenty on the Dams Raid, his 21st birthday occurring on 27th May, ten days later) his DSO and DFC, with a tour with Guy Gibson's 106 Squadron – a tour of 36 ops.

Joe McCarthy, a member of the RCAF was in fact an American, from New York, was twenty-three, and also held the DSO and DFC. He had flown on the first 1,000 Bomber raids while still at OTU, then gone on to complete a tour with 106 Squadron, then started a second tour with 97 Squadron before being picked to fly with 617. Geoff Rice, DFC, twenty-six, had flown his tour with 57 Squadron but on the Dams Raid had had the misfortune to lose his bomb when he hit the sea on his way out to the enemy coast and had to abort. Les Munro, DSO, DFC was a New Zealander aged

10

twenty-four. A member of the RNZAF he flew his tour with 97 Squadron. Bill Townsend, aged twenty-two, from Gloucester, had won the DFM with 49 Squadron, and been awarded the Conspicuous Gallantry Medal for the Dams attack, and had recently been commissioned. Ken Brown, a Canadian, had also won the CGM for the Dams Raid. He was twenty-two and had only just begun a tour with 44 Squadron before coming to 617. Two pilots who had missed the actual raid, had been Harold Wilson, who had joined the squadron from 57 Squadron and who was twenty-eight, and 23-year-old Bill Divall, also in from 57 Squadron.

Early in July two more crews arrived to fill the vacancies. One was that of Squadron Leader G. Holden, DSO, DFC and bar, who was the squadron's new Commanding Officer designate, and Pilot Officer B.W. Clayton, DFC, CGM. George Holden, twenty-nine years old, came from 57 Squadron, and had previously flown with 78 and 102 Squadrons. Bunny Clayton had previously flown with 44 Squadron.

Although grounded, Guy Gibson remained with the squadron for several days, during which time the crews continued to train while the fate of their squadron was decided upon by Headquarters Bomber Command. They also exchanged their specially modified Lancasters, used for the Dams Raid, for the basic models as used by other Main Force bomber squadrons.

*

It was quickly established that 617 should undertake attacks on special targets – targets where the experienced men would hopefully achieve decisive results. The first such targets were not in Germany but Italy. The first attack was scheduled for 15th July. Twelve Lancasters would attempt to knock out an electric power plant at Aquata Scriva (Ciseago), fifteen miles north-west of Milan, and a transformer station at San Polo D'Enza (Brugherio), eight miles nearer Milan.

The first six were led by acting Wing Commander Holden, with the crews of Flight Lieutenant Harold Wilson, Pilot Officer Bill Townsend, Pilot Officer Ken Brown, Flight Lieutenant R.A. Allsebrook, DSO, DFC, another new arrival, and finally Bunny Clayton. Allsebrook had flown over fifty trips with 49 Squadron.

The second formation, led by Squadron Leader David Maltby, consisted of Flight Lieutenant Mick Martin, Pilot Officer Geoff Rice (who had lost his bomb when he hit the sea on the Dams Raid), Flight Lieutenant Les Munro (who had been forced to abandon his part in the raid when his intercom was knocked out), Squadron Leader Joe McCarthy and Sergeant Bill Divall, who had like Wilson missed the famous raid. Gibson had wanted to lead the 15th July raid himself but permission was refused. Instead, all he could do was to wave them off from the edge of the runway.

The targets were important. With the battle for Sicily well advanced, a landing upon the mainland of Italy was expected. With Mussolini's dictatorship looking decidedly shaky, a crippling blow against the power which supplied Italy's electric railway system would be nicely timed. However, it was a long trip with no hope of getting back to England. Instead, the force would fly south to land at Blida, twenty miles from Algiers in North Africa.

The trip was unopposed. The first wave took off between 10 and 10.25 p.m., arriving over the target at 3.24 a.m. They found it obscured by haze and had to bomb blind. Bill Townsend made three bombing runs in an attempt to positively identify the target, then let his fourteen-pound 500 bombs go from 800 feet. They fell south of the plant but did hit an armoured train which caused smoke to rise high into the night sky. Another train was hit by Ralph Allsebrook in the same area although his Lancaster was slightly damaged by flak. Flight Lieutenant Wilson's bomber was also hit as he and the others all made runs by guesswork. Ken Brown decided to bomb the secondary target, putting his bombs onto a military barracks near Genoa.

Meanwhile, the second group also found difficulty locating their target through the haze. Despite this, several bombs were believed to have straddled and hit the transformer station as blue electric flashes were seen. David Maltby put most of his bombs into the target but one 500-pounder and an incendiary bomb failed to release. His bomb-aimer later got rid of them on the Genoa–Spezia railway at Sestri Levante.

Flak hit the Lancaster of Les Munro which punctured a tyre, hit the bomb-aimer's panel and inflicted cuts to the man's face. Another aircraft was damaged but this was from bomb splinters – McCarthy and crew, bombing from 800 feet.

All twelve bombers landed at Blida, a pre-war French base, shortly after 7 a.m., Les Munro making a one-wheeled landing at 8.20.

It was something of an anti-climax, for although they felt the bombs had hit the targets, the results were far from positive. If only flares or some kind of illumination had been possible, then they felt they could really have achieved impressive results, especially in view of the light flak they had encountered. As it turned out, these were prophetic thoughts that were later to bear fruit. Bomber Command itself was beginning to perfect target marking and target illumination – the Pathfinder Force having already been created. It was still improving its techniques.

Part of the payload taken to Blida for the men stationed there were kegs of beer. In the evening, the 617 crews went into the town for a drink and a meal at a French restaurant. The waiter was named Louis who had been taught a little English by the Eighth Army soldiers. As the evening wore on so did the crews' high spirits. Dougie Warwick, Divall's Canadian navigator, played a very good 'Boogie Woogie' on the piano. They also managed to buy some champagne to bring to England, but only after showing their 'Le Canadien' shoulder flashes. The three-mile journey back to the airfield seemed more like six and Dougie found the greatest difficulty navigating into his mosquito netting!

The twelve aircraft left Blida on the 24th, bombing the harbour at Leghorn on the way. Cloud over this Italian port was quite heavy with haze below but the docks were identified and bombed. Joe McCarthy claimed a direct hit on what he thought was an oil storage depot. Allsebrook also hit an oil dump, but over the target his starboard outer engine failed and he could not maintain height; he finally arrived back at Scampton on three engines.

Another experienced crew arrived on the 26th, captained by Flight Lieutenant E.E.G. Youseman, DFC, aged twenty-one. Ted Youseman had flown forty-three ops with 214 Squadron and, of his crew, four had been decorated.

It was back to Italy on the 29th, but not to drop bombs but leaflets. These were intended to help persuade the Italians to end their war. Nine aircraft went to the towns of Bologna, Milan, Genoa and Turin, and again they continued south to Blida. With the exception of McCarthy, delayed through engine trouble (he returned on 5th August), the Lancasters returned to England on the first day of August loaded with fresh fruit and wine.

The squadron's first casualty since May occurred on the afternoon of 5th August, when Flight Lieutenant Kellaway, in Lancaster ED765 (letter M), crashed at Ashley Walk bombing range whilst taking part in a tactical exercise. During a low level flight his bomber was caught in the slipstream of another aircraft, struck the ground and caught fire. They were experimenting with a spinning bomb to be used against shipping. In the event, however, the bomb was never used. The wireless operator, Pilot Officer S. Harris, recorded:

> We approached the Ashley Walk range at low-level, our target a simulated viaduct. We dropped our dummy spinning bomb (Wallis) in an attempt to roll it against the arches of the viaduct, all previous high level bombing attacks (against such targets) being ineffective. The weather was bad, and flying at 60 feet we were suddenly hit by a gust of wind[1] which caused us to drop suddenly and fly into the ground.

Kellaway, Harris, Pilot Officer R. Drury (the bomb-aimer) and one of the gunners, Flight Sergeant H. Temple, were all injured. Harris had to undergo plastic surgery and never flew on operations again. Temple returned to 617 in November 1944, crewed with Flight Lieutenant Pryor, and became a prisoner of war when they were shot down in January 1945.

Guy Gibson left England for Canada on a lecture tour at the beginning of August, and George Holden officially took command of 617. Gibson had flown on just one operation since the Dams Raid, and had now been totally grounded. Returning from Canada Gibson held various ground positions until he moved to HQ 54 Base at Coningsby in August 1944. He managed to fly on a couple of missions but was not given an operational command. Having been allowed to fly just one more op on 19th September, he was shot down and killed in a Mosquito as Master Bomber. He and his navigator were buried at Steenbergen, Holland.

[1] The official report says slipstream.

CHAPTER TWO

On the Move

A warning order to move to RAF Coningsby, $7\frac{1}{2}$ miles south-west of Horncastle in Lincolnshire, came on 11th August. Coningsby's daytime land-marks for aircrews were a 100 foot windmill in the local village, Tattershall Castle and Boston Stump, some 250 feet high, $10\frac{1}{2}$ miles away. An advanced party left Scampton on the 25th, the main move coming five days later. 617 was to share the new base with 619 Squadron and would fly several operations with them over the next year or so.

Training took up the squadron's time over the next couple of weeks, much of it low level practice at Wainfleet bombing range in cooperation with Mosquito aircraft of 418 and 605 Squadrons. Low level flying had been greatly improved by the production of radio altimeters which could be set at a desired height – usually 75 to 100 feet – which then gave the pilot an immediate visual indication if he flew below that height. Unbeknown to the crews was that this was in preparation for an attack upon one of Bomber Command's old targets – the Dortmund-Ems Canal.

This canal ran to the north of Münster near Ladbergen and consisted of a shallow waterway approximately $12\frac{1}{2}$ feet deep and 100 feet wide at water level. This canal was just one part of Germany's system of inland waterways, yet it was the only link by water between the Ruhr and Eastern Germany or the North Sea and Baltic. Its barges carried millions of tons of freight to and from the factories of the Ruhr, especially valuable iron ore from Sweden.

It had been attacked on numerous occasions since 1940 but although it was vulnerable from air attack at several points where there were either viaducts or embankments over low lying ground, it could be repaired almost as quickly as it was damaged. In August

1940, Squadron Leader R.A.B. Learoyd, flying a Hampden of 49 Squadron, had received the VC for an attack upon it, in the face of heavy AA fire.

The point chosen for 617's attack was at Greven where the canal divided into two branches. It was planned to mount the raid on the first suitable date after 11th September, the 14th being the night finally set. To cause the maximum damage, the Lancasters would carry a 12,000 lb HC bomb. Eight Lancasters would take part, supported by six Mosquitos of Fighter Command plus two reserve Lancasters.

The operation called for particularly careful planning as the more vulnerable parts of the canal were heavily defended, many of which came within artillery zones of important industrial towns. As the bombing called for a hit within forty feet of the canal bank, it necessitated a low level approach with good visibility, i.e.: moonlight! The force was divided into two, each with three Mosquitos as escort who would deal with flak and searchlights.

The force set off on the evening of the 14th but a Mosquito reconnaissance aircraft that flew out ahead of them reported that the weather was too bad over the target area, so the force was recalled. Squadron Leader Maltby (in JA981 'N') turned his aircraft at 0.45 a.m. but in doing so he hit the sea with a wingtip and went in. Whether he was caught in a slipstream, had an aircraft malfunction or simply misjudged his height we will never know. Flight Lieutenant Dave Shannon saw the crash and circled the area for 2½ hours until an air-sea rescue craft arrived, but only the body of David Maltby was ever found.

He and his crew were sadly missed, not least by his ground crew. To have survived so much only to die in this way seemed so tragic. He and his crew were the first of the Dam Buster survivors to be lost.

The next night 617 tried again. The operation had to be done and they now owed it to Maltby and his crew to finish it. The force crossed the enemy coast in two groups and flew by different routes to reach the canal where it ran from north to south for a number of miles. Leading the first group was George Holden, with Martin, Knight and Wilson. Allsebrook followed with Shannon, Rice and Divall. Visibility was excellent which made navigation easy. Some twenty miles from the target, light flak opened up on the first group which hit Holden's Lancaster in a petrol tank. The bomber hit the ground at Nordhorn-Altendorf, crashing into a farm house in the Hesperweg, where it and the 12,000 lb bomb blew up. The farmer's wife and the Lancaster crew all died in the explosion. It was George Holden's thirtieth birthday.

The formation broke up to skirt Nordhorn and became separated owing to a thick ground haze. The crews remained in radio communication with each other, however, and reached the canal without further incident, although it was only possible to make out the canal when vertically over it. As planned, Allsebrook – the Deputy Leader – dropped a parachute beacon, followed by a second one, a 'safeguard' beacon, two miles to the east, but owing to the haze they were not seen. Incendiary bombs carried in reserve for marking were also dropped but they could only be seen when directly over them.

In the terrible visibility around the target, at times in the order of only 500 yards, a prolonged and determined search was carried out by the seven crews. In these conditions it was easy to fly a wider orbit than intended, which allowed local flak positions to engage the Lancasters overhead. The Mosquitos engaged some of the guns but they too had difficulty in making out details on the ground.

Only two Lancasters were able to locate and bomb the target, one bomb falling into the canal, its explosion throwing up a water spout to around 1,500 feet. This Lancaster was flown by Mick Martin, the second by Shannon, whose bomb exploded on the towpath. Neither saw any material damage. Meanwhile four of the other Lancasters were hit and shot down in the general area.

Les Knight had been detailed as sixth to bomb and had been instructed to fly a square course of one minute legs while waiting his turn to bomb. As they were flying the first leg, another aircraft was seen ahead, Knight, therefore, flew longer on the first and third legs and less on the second and fourth so as to avoid the other aeroplane. After completing one circuit in this manner the canal had not been observed, so they held their course a few seconds longer.

Suddenly the bomb aimer yelled, 'Look out, high ground ahead!'

Les Knight pulled back the control column instantly but too late.

17

They hit the tops of some trees which jarred the Lancaster and punctured both radiators of the port engines. It is possible that the fins and rudder were also damaged as Knight had difficulty in controlling the machine. Being unable to climb, he requested permission from Martin to jettison his bomb.

Having got rid of the bomb he set course for home and was able to reach 1,500 feet. Almost immediately, however, the port inner engine started to leave a trail of white smoke and the flight engineer feathered it. He had no sooner done so when the port outer engine began to show similar symptoms and was also feathered. Knight was able to maintain a height of 1,200 feet at 140 mph but with both port engines out of action he was finding it difficult to fly on a straight course.

With the rear turret unserviceable as a result of the port engine being feathered (which controlled the turret's hydraulics), the gunner, Sergeant Harry O'Brien, came forward to the bomb aimer's compartment where he sat facing his pilot and pulled hard on the port rudder bar with all his strength, while Knight pushed with his left foot. They continued like this for twenty minutes, and as long as they kept up this pressure it was possible to maintain a fairly straight course but when they relaxed for a moment the aircraft veered off course.

Soon the two starboard engines began to show signs of overheating, so the port inner engine was restarted. It ran normally for about 30 seconds before starting to smoke. It was feathered again and the outer engine tried but with the same result. Knight said he thought he could hold the aircraft long enough for them to reach the North Sea but it would be necessary for them to bale out over Holland. The navigator, Sidney Hobday, told Knight when they had reached a point about thirty miles inside the Dutch frontier and he gave the order to bale out. Bob Kellow, the wireless operator, had been continuously reporting their progress back to base. He now reported that they were abandoning the aircraft.

Flying Officer Johnson, the bomb aimer and O'Brien were first out. They left through the forward escape hatch, followed by Sergeant Ray Grayston, the engineer, Hobday and then Kellow. As Kellow passed Knight, the latter signified that all was as well as could be expected. When coming down in his parachute, Kellow saw the Lancaster pass overhead still flying level, and later saw it burning on the ground. The front and mid-upper gunners, Sergeants Fred Sutherland and Woollard, both left by the side door. Woollard was not a regular member of the crew. He landed safely, evaded capture and later got himself back to England.

Flying Officer Johnson was jammed in the nose of the aircraft for a short while but finally pulled himself free. He landed in a field of sugar beet about six miles from Almelo. He had just landed when the Lancaster came back over his head, only about fifty feet up, then crashed into the next field and burst into flames. It was 3.46 a.m., 16th September, near Den Ham, about sixteen miles south-east of Zwolle.

The aircraft had come down after clipping some trees which still bear signs of the crash, while others still show signs from the fire. The field had a small wire fence across it which gave Les Knight no chance for any kind of belly landing. Baron Van Pallandte, with a friend, went immediately to the burning Lancaster but they were unable to help Knight who must have died immediately. He related that the pilot had tried very hard to land, hopping over trees in an attempt to get down. He also stated at the time, 'I know and can say that he was a very brave fellow.' Knight had kept the bomber flying long enough for his crew to jump, but in doing so had paid the price so many bomber captains had to pay for their final brave acts. Les Knight[1] was given a wonderful funeral and was buried in Den Ham by the local Dutch people. So yet another pilot from the Dams Raid was lost.

Sidney Hobday landed in a tree. With his parachute caught in the branches he managed to free himself and get down. When he revisited the area after the war he was given part of his parachute harness; it still had his name on it.

Before baling out he had told the others to head for the south-west, and had also shouted to Knight, 'Come on, Les!'

Knight's reponse was, 'Jump, God bless you.'

Once on the ground, Hobday saw in the distance a grey German patrol car. The occupants did not see him but a farmhand saw him, asking, 'Tommy?'

Hobday said, 'No, RAF.'

[1] Awarded Mention in Despatches (Post.).

The farmhand did not quite understand so Hobday picked up a piece of wood and wrote in the dirt, 'RAF'. With this the man said, 'Oh, Air-ah-eff.' He shook his hand and bade him farewell and continued on his way.

He later met a couple who spoke English who told him they had met another Englishman. Their description was of Bob Kellow. They took Hobday to a wood, gave him some apples and told him to wait. After a while a man came with a package containing some civilian clothes. He changed and gave the man his uniform. He was eventually passed along an escape line, via Paris, across the Pyrenees into Spain to reach Gibraltar. He flew back to the UK in time for Christmas. The Dutch had asked him to arrange for radio equipment to be dropped should he get home, and this was duly done.

Flight Lieutenant Harold Wilson crashed between 3 and 4 a.m. at Recke-Obersteinbeck, near Ladbergen. He had flown low over the target when his aircraft was hit by a 2 cm flak gun. Wilson made a belly landing and after about fifteen minutes his machine exploded. A local farmer heard cries for help and on his way to help, was blown over by the explosion and severely injured. A large proportion of the Lancaster was on the southern side of the Mittelland Canal; the rear turret with the body of the dead gunner was found on the northern side. All eight men died and their bodies were taken away for burial by the Germans.

Flight Lieutenant Ralph Allsebrook, who had taken over when Holden was brought down, crashed at Bergeshovede in the German district of Recklenberg. He had dropped his own bomb and then directed two others onto the target before he was seen hit and on fire.

After making his run, he had called Mick Martin on the W/T, 'Hold on a minute until I get out of this,' (he meant the light flak), and was then heard to say, 'I am returning to base.' Martin then took over as leader.

Allsebrook and his crew were buried in an Evangelical Cemetery at Horsteb.

*

The failure of the operation was primarily due to a belt of haze which, contrary to the weather forecast, was found in the area surrounding the target, making it impossible for the crews to keep track of their exact position. This in turn made them overfly flak positions while searching for the target. As for the target, it remained undamaged and as formidable as ever.

It had been a total disaster. Four Lancasters and their crews had gone for a nil result. The loss of its squadron commander too was bad enough, but his crew, with the exception of the engineer and rear gunner, had been Gibson's crew on the Dams Raid. Taerum, Hutchinson, Spam Spafford, Deering – all had perished with George Holden in the crash. It must have been a terrific blow to Gibson when the news reached him. Flying Officer Dave Rodger of Joe McCarthy's crew remembers trying to get word to Bob Hutchinson's fiancée that he was missing. He was down for an operation on the night of the 16th and so finally had to tell his mother. This he hated doing but he could not find anyone else at home to tell before take-off time.

Mick Martin was promoted to squadron leader immediately and given temporary command of 617. Had it not been for the fact that he had only been a flight lieutenant, which meant a jump of two ranks to wing commander, he might well have been given full command. Martin himself was all for going back to the canal the next night but another operation had already been planned.

So, despite the severe losses, 617 was briefed to attack another special target the next night, the 16th. This time it was in Southern France, the Anthéor Viaduct, near St Raphael just along the coast from Cannes. It carried a double track of the Marseille–Genoa railways across the mouth of a small river, seven miles east of St Raphael, near the village of Anthéor. It consisted of nine arches built on a curve and stood immediately on the shore line of the Mediterrannean. It was 540 feet long, 185 feet high, and each arch had a span of about 29 feet; each pier was eight feet thick. It was estimated that 14,400 tons of military supplies or other goods entered Italy each day over the viaduct and went straight to the Italian front.

As 617 Squadron was so depleted, it joined forces with 619 Squadron and was led by its CO, Wing Commander Abercromby. There were six aircraft from each unit; 617 consisted of Bunny

Clayton, Ted Youseman, Les Munro, David Wilson.[1] Joe McCarthy and Ken Brown.

Take-off was between 7.57 p.m. and 8.18, the crews arriving over the distant target shortly after 1 a.m. The first to bomb were Youseman and McCarthy at 1.15. Each Lancaster carried seven 1,000-lb bombs. Youseman dropped his on the first run while McCarthy made one dummy run before dropping them on the second, both loads from 300 feet. The rest took their turns and bombed with the exception of Clayton who suffered icing problems and had to jettison his load.

The attack was another failure, for the viaduct was left undamaged although some damage was done to the railway lines. This however was repaired within 24 hours.

Things were not looking too bright for the squadron. In two raids it had failed to hit its assigned targets and lost four crews, plus another during an aborted mission. For a unique unit that had reaped so much kudos and prestige just four months earlier, 617's place within Bomber Command must have been questioned.

Nevertheless, replacement crews began to arrive. Martin had the job of interviewing them and some were far from keen to join. 617 was beginning to be known as a suicide unit and crews felt their already slim chances of completing a normal tour of ops were far better with their own squadron than flying with 617.

The first replacement crew arrived on 5th October. This was Flying Officer Willsher and his crew from 61 Squadron who had just completed fifteen operations. Four days later an accident occurred while a low flying exercise was being carried out by Warrant Officer Bull (ED886 'O'). They were flying at 25-30 feet. The bomb aimer, Norman Batey, was in the nose map-reading when suddenly they hit the top of a tree. Bull caught sight of it just before they hit and had pulled up slightly but all the perspex was shattered, injuring Batey's face while his maps were all blasted back down the aircraft. The flight engineer assisted the injured man to the rest bed while the wireless operator put a dressing on his injured head. Despite his flying helmet, Batey had received a nasty wound which bled freely, but he was the only one hurt.

[1] F/L D.J.B. Wilson, not H.S. Wilson who had been lost the previous night.

Flying Officer G.S. Stout transferred from 619 Squadron on the 21st, and the next day Pilot Officer Nick Ross and crew arrived from 103 Squadron. A few days later 617 received a visit from the AOC 5 Group, Air-Vice Marshal the Hon R.A. Cochrane, when Coningsby had a formal inspection.

The month ended with another arrival, Flying Officer Paddy Gingles in from 432 Squadron.

Nick Ross had got off to a bad start with 617 when he too hit a tree on the 30th, but he got away with it.

During this period Dick Willsher had also experienced difficulty while on a low level exercise. With most squadrons, low flying usually meant no lower than 300 feet, with 617 it meant no higher than 50 feet! Mick Martin had told him, 'Don't, if you can help it, fly over trees or haystacks; fly alongside them!'

On this trip, since he was inexperienced compared with the other 617 pilots, Willsher decided to let everyone else land first, but by the time his turn came, a mist had set in over the airfield and he was finding it difficult to get down.

Then a voice came over the radio, 'Hang on, Dick, I'll come up, and get you down.' It was Martin.

He took off, guided Willsher down and had actually touched down again himself before Willsher had reached the end of the runway.

CHAPTER THREE

The Cheshire Era

Geoffrey Leonard Cheshire assumed command of the squadron on
10th November 1943. Already something of a legend within
Bomber Command, Leonard Cheshire was a highly decorated and
experienced bomber captain and acknowledged leader.

He was twenty-six years of age, born in Chester, and had been
educated at Stowe and Merton College, Oxford, where he had
studied law. While at Oxford his interests turned to flying and he
joined the University Air Squadron in 1937. Later that year he was
commissioned in the RAF Volunteer Reserve, and as such he was
mobilised at the outbreak of war. Completing his flying training he
received his 'wings' in December 1939, and upon completion of his
OTU training, joined 102 Squadron, flying Whitley bombers. He
stayed with this unit for five months, bombing various German
targets, including Berlin. On the night of 12/13th November 1940,
during a raid on Cologne, his aircraft was severely damaged by
flak, one piece of shrapnel detonating a flare inside the Whitley
which in turn ripped open the side of the fuselage. Regaining
control, he went on to bomb the target, then flew the bomber home.
For this effort he received an immediate DSO.

Completing his first tour in January 1941 he immediately
undertook a second tour, this time with 35 Squadron, flying the
new Halifax four-engined bombers. During 1941, while with 35
Squadron he was awarded firstly the DFC and later a bar to his
DSO for 'outstanding leadership and skill on operations'. Ending
his second tour he became an instructor at a Heavy Conversion
Unit, but still managed to get in four trips, including the first 1,000
Bomber Raid.

In August 1942 he returned to operational flying, being given

24

command of 76 Squadron, the unit his younger brother Christopher had been with before he was shot down over Berlin and became a prisoner of war in August 1941. With 76 he gained a second bar to his DSO, in April 1942, and with the rank of Wing Commander was the most highly decorated pilot in the RAF.

The following year, at twenty-five the youngest group captain in the RAF, Leonard Cheshire was given command of RAF Station, Marston Moor. His desire to return to operational duties came later that year with the vacancy in 617 Squadron, although he had to revert to the rank of Wing Commander to do so.

His posting came as 617 was about to have another crack at the Anthéor Viaduct, detailed for 11th November. Cheshire arrived a few days later, and so it was Micky Martin who led the squadron that night. This time each Lancaster carried one 12,000-lb bomb.

Flight Lieutenant Youseman took off first at 6.15 p.m., followed in order by O'Shaughnessy, Munro, Rice, Shannon, Bull, Martin, Clayton, Wilson, Brown and another newcomer, Flight Lieutenant R.S.D. Kearns, DFC, DFM. As he took off, Dave Shannon's aircraft had an engine failure and had to abort.

Over the target, Martin dropped his bomb from 5,800 feet and it was seen falling on the railway line left of the viaduct. Several light guns and searchlights were encountered in the target area but Les Munro calmly made two dummy runs before his bomb went down to explode half a mile to the north-east of the target. Kearns, a former Pathfinder pilot, dropped his bomb from 8,000 feet but it undershot by about sixty yards. To this day, Warrant Officer Joe Dacey still remembers hearing the explosion above all the other noises. As he went in, Wilson saw some small ships four miles out in the bay. He dropped his bomb on the viaduct and it overshot by thirty yards. Youseman's overshot by 150 yards, and O'Shaughnessy's bomb landed to the right of the railway bridge. He was also fired on from one of the ships. Bull's bomb was seen to make a direct hit on or near the tunnel entrance of the railway. Bunny Clayton's bomb overshot by fifty yards and it is not clear where Brown's bomb landed.

Warrant Officer Stefan Onacia, Ken Brown's Canadian bomb aimer, identified the target and Brown agreed, but on turning for the run up they saw a similar railway at Agay and bombed this, although Onacia saw a white gleam which he thought was the viaduct. Visual evidence seemed to confirm a hit on the eastern end of the embankment, possibly near the tunnel entrance.

It became apparent after debriefing that the similarity of the coastal bay adjacent to the viaduct with nearby Agay, had caused some crews to mis-identify the target. It had not been brought to the attention of the crews earlier as it was assumed that most had been there before, whereas in fact only five of the ten who flew out had flown on the earlier operation.

Once again the viaduct had survived. Fifteen people nearby to the viaduct had been killed and a few more injured. Unscathed, the Lancasters again headed south to Blida.

The force left for Rabat, north-west Africa, fifty miles from Casablanca, on 15th November, but not before they had loaded up the Lancasters with Christmas parcels from various RAF personnel at Blida, for their families in England. They left Rabat on the 18th, flying low level to England along the coast of Portugal and skirting the Bay of Biscay. Unhappily one Lancaster failed to make it. Ted Youseman was seen to ditch into the sea off Portugal and was last heard of at 5.55 a.m. when 75 miles south-west of Brest. He and his crew were assumed lost.

When the others arrived home, they were told by their groundcrews that they had a new CO by the name of Cheshire. The crews' first concern was how would the new boss take to the idea of them bringing back the Christmas gifts and parcels, but they need not have worried. Not only did he approve but arranged for trucks to take the parcels to Lincoln Post Office. Joe Dacey remembers bringing back some bananas for his nephew who had not seen such fruit before.

Joe also recalls an event at about this time concerning Kearns. He and his crew were flying an air test at about 12,000 feet, when suddenly all four engines stopped. With the exception of Kearns, the crew panicked, wondering what had happened. Kearns then informed them that he had feathered them and that provided they all re-started, he would pass the kite as serviceable! Fortunately the engines did start although the groundcrew were not over happy at the state of the batteries when they landed.

On the same occasion, Joe was doing a stint of flying practice when the nose started to drop. The more he pulled on the control column the more the nose appeared to go down. More than a little alarmed, he finally glanced at Kearns and saw him grinning, having trimmed the machine nose down as Joe had pulled on the stick.

There was a complete contrast for the squadron early in December when McCarthy, Clayton, Bull and Pilot Officer Weeden were sent off for special operations duties with 138/161 Special Duties Squadrons. Cheshire had been requested to supply four crews for low level duties at Tempsford – a 'hush-hush' airfield where aircraft flew agents and Resistance people into occupied Europe. He chose the four, led by McCarthy. Two days later Bull and Weeden were both posted missing.

All four Lancasters had flown out on the night of 10th December to drop ammunition and guns to the Resistance, near Doullens in France. Bull, in ED886 'O',[1] crossed the Channel in bright moonlight, crossed the French coast at 10.15 p.m., dropping down to 500 feet. A few miles north of the River Somme and heading towards the dropping site at Doullens, Bull let down to fifty feet as he flew over the town. A battery of about eight guns opened up from the left. Both air gunners, Flight Sergeant McWilliams and Sergeant Stewart returned fire but then McWilliams heard a 'crump' in the bomb bay as the Lancaster was hit. The aircraft caught fire, the port petrol tank being well alight. Bull handled the aircraft excellently, trying to gain height for his crew to bale out and succeeded in reaching 800 feet. He gave the order to stand by, also sent out the emergency warning call sign, 'Abracadabra', then the aircraft was heading for the ground nearly out of control.

The navigator, Sergeant Chamberlain, was in trouble when his parachute partially opened when he caught it on a lever projecting from the pilot's seat. Batey, the bomb aimer, grabbed his own 'chute, snapped it quickly in position and tried to tell Bull he was jumping, but found the intercom dead. He then ripped off the cover from the escape hatch and lifted it to throw it out, when he saw McWilliams coming out of his turret. The escape hatch was caught by the slipstream and jammed when he tried to throw it out, so he kicked it with his right foot, but only succeeded in jamming his foot between the hatch and the frame. A second quick thrust and the hatch fell away, but so too did his boot. Batey rolled forward through the opening and when his parachute cracked open saw he was very close to the ground. He landed in a ploughed field which, owing to the wintry frost was pretty hard and gave his back a nasty jolt which caused him some discomfort for several weeks. He guessed his location to be in the area between Boulogne and St Pol.

McWilliams also got down and when descending saw the Lancaster go down, burning furiously. After it crashed there were two large explosions and the wreck burnt for about twenty minutes.

Despite his partially opened parachute, Sergeant Chamberlain got away safely and on landing he too found the ground very hard. He stuffed his 'chute into a haystack, then met up with Batey and another crew member, Sergeant Wiltshire. They decided to make for Paris and spent the next few hours crossing fields etc, keeping well away from roads as much as possible. They finally reached a small village where they decided to rest in the tower of the local church. On arrival they found a sleeping German sentry, and decided to get away as quickly as they could. They had not gone far, however, before a shot was fired. They dropped to the ground and were just about to rise and make a run for it when a German soldier in a black uniform appeared, wearing the insignia of the death's head. It turned out that they had been captured by an SS Panzer division based in the village.

For the next two days they were moved from place to place until they ended up at Amiens Prison, (famous later for the RAF attack in February 1944). Here they found their pilot, 'Chuffy' Bull, in a truck in which they were all about to be taken away. Bull had injured both his legs in landing, for while the others had all baled out about 700 feet, he must have jumped at about 400 to 500 feet. However, the bad news was that Sergeant Johnny Stewart, their wireless operator, who had been in the mid-upper turret, and the rear gunner, Flight Sergeant Don Thorpe, had both been killed. Later, while in a German POW camp, they heard that McWilliams had evaded capture and got back to England, via Gibraltar, on 22nd February 1944.

Flying Officer Gordon Weeden, RCAF, and his crew, were less

fortunate than Bull's. They too must have been caught at low level by German AA fire, for they too failed to return, and all seven men were killed. Joe McCarthy added to the disaster by not even finding the dropping area. He and Bunny Clayton tried again the next night and this time they succeeded.

It was France again on 16th December, when nine aircraft were detailed to attack a construction works at Flixecourt/Domant-en-Ponthieu, in Northern France. The target was to be marked by Pathfinder Mosquitos, but the marking proved inaccurate, being 35 yards off centre, and consequently the target was not hit. Later recce photographs showed 617's bombing error to be only 94 yards, that there were no bombs more than 150 yards from the markers and that two had been within 30 yards.

Failure in marking caused 617 to return from an attempted raid on an armaments works at Liège in Belgium on the 20th. German night fighters were reported in the area, but flak had been light; only a short flurry of AA fire was met halfway to the target. However, Geoff Rice's Lancaster was caught by a night fighter which set his bomber on fire.

Rice remembered nothing after giving the order to bale out. At approximately 8.30 the following morning he regained consciousness and found himself in a wood with his parachute hanging from a tree. The wreckage of his aircraft was scattered around, his wrist was broken and he had a severe cut over his left eye. Staggering from the wood, he met three farm labourers and after he had told them he was British, they took him to a farm. Sometime later he was taken to a doctor who set his wrist in plaster.

Over the next few weeks he was moved from town to town in 'safe' houses organised by the Belgian Resistance until he ended up in Brussels at the end of January 1944. In April he went by train to Antwerp, but finally, on the 28th, he was reported to the Secret Police and captured. He remained a prisoner until his release one year later. He had been on the run for over four months. The rest of his crew were killed in the crash, although the Red Cross later reported that Sergeant Chester Gowrie, RCAF, the wireless operator, had been shot by the Germans. Geoff Rice, a founder member of the squadron, died in 1981.

Cloud prevented another French target being hit three days before Christmas. Then on the 30th it was back for another try against Flixecourt/Domant. With 8 Group Pathfinder Mosquitos marking the target, ten Lancasters flew out to hit what was now known to be a V1 flying bomb launching site, called by the British 'ski' sites because of their shape.

The Mosquitos dropped yellow route markers north of the target and Green Target Indicators (T.I) which contained three red candles. One aircraft of 617 had its bomb release fail but the others all let go their 12,000-pounders and considerable damage was caused to the target, including two ski ramps, a small rectangular building and some excavations on the north side of the site.

A V1 site was again the target for the squadron's first raid of 1944, on 4th January. Cheshire was not at all happy with recent attempts to mark the target by 8 Group's Mosquitos and felt that 617 might just as well provide their own marking. Eleven Lancasters took part in this operation and floating flares were dropped from 12,000 feet. Cloud was again the major problem. The Station Commander of Coningsby, Group Captain Anthony Evans-Evans, took the occasion to fly with Cheshire. It was to be his last chance for 617 Squadron were about to move from his station.[1]

---

[1] Group Captain A. Evans-Evans was killed in action in February 1945.

CHAPTER FOUR

Final Home

The squadron moved to what was to become its final wartime home on the 8th January 1944. RAF Woodhall Spa was six miles south-west of Horncastle and its permanent landmark was Tattershall Castle and woods. The station was only about ten miles from Coningsby and the officers' mess was at the Petwood Hotel, just a little way from the airfield. 619 were also at Woodhall Spa.

The move heralded the arrival of Pilot Officer G.S. Stout, Lieutenant Nick Knilans, DSO DFC and Flying Officer Cooper, with their crews, all from 619 Squadron. Nick Knilans, although in the USAAF, had in fact started in the RCAF, enlisting in October 1941. He transferred to the American Air Force in November 1943 but continued to fly with the RAF to finish his tour. Before the war he had been a private detective in Chicago, and when he arrived in England and was asked why he had come, replied: 'To bring happiness to the children of Europe.' He spent eight months at Woodhall Spa with 619, and his room at the hotel, No 32, looks very much the same now as it did then. He had won the DSO with 619 following seventeen bombing operations, but in particular for one raid when with both of his gunners hit, one dead and one wounded, he carried on to bomb the target. On a similar occasion he was attacked by Ju88 night fighters. One his crew shot down and despite damage to his Lancaster he again carried on to the target.

In recent low level attacks on V1 sites, 617 had experienced radio jamming by the Germans. At this time a new frequency was given them and new crystals arranged. They were also given help by various Fighter Command control stations who could warn them when enemy aircraft approached from anything up to 180 miles. This cover began at Beachy Head on the south coast and could range from a height of 20,000 down to 1,000 feet.

On an unlucky 13th January, Wing Commander Cheshire hit a flock of birds when he took off. They were plovers that suddenly flew up in front of him. He just had time to lower his seat, put his head down below the level of the windscreen before the birds hit; then he flew on instruments. King, his engineer, was injured but Cheshire landed back safely. A party of men later went out to the runway and produced twenty of the dead birds for dinner in the mess that evening.

There was another flying accident a week later, on a training flight. Six aircraft took off on a low level bombing practice during which Flight Lieutenant O'Shaughnessy, flying at sixty feet, and while intent on his instruments, appeared to lose control of the Lancaster and hit a sea wall on Snettisham beach. It was just 8 p.m. and the Lancaster (ED918'F') caught fire and burnt out. Of those on board, O'Shaughnessy was killed, so too was Flying Officer Arthur Holding. Pilot Officer A.J. Ward, DFC was slightly injured and Flying Officer G.A. Kendrick badly injured; he later flew again but was killed in January 1945.

On the 21st it was back to the ski sites in the Pas de Calais, and they had help from the Fighter Control Stations. After a successful attack, Cheshire remained over the area but was informed that enemy aircraft were coming up fairly rapidly. He turned for home, climbing, and was clear of the hostile coast before they reached him.

Flight Sergeant Woollard arrived back on the 24th, having been shot down with Les Knight back in September. On the same day Squadron Leader Patrick Moyna of the RAF Film Unit paid a visit to the squadron. He was to feature greatly in 617's future operations. He was expecting to be given little help from Cheshire, for Moyna had been vainly trying for some time to get people interested in his Film Unit. With some relief he found Cheshire keen on trying to photograph actual operations.

The Pas de Calais saw 617 again on the 25th. Another ski site had been located in a wood, covered with netting. There was no opposition and twelve aircraft bombed the area.

On 8th February, 617 went for the Gnôme-Rhône aircraft factory at Limoges, 200 miles south-west of Paris. It was a modern

32

plant, built in 1939, which specialised in aero-engine repairs. It remained empty for some months and in June 1941, Gnôme and Rhône were allotted space in the premises; owing to delays in tooling, however, production did not begin until August 1942. Research was also carried out there, and it employed some 500 French workers. This latter consideration had caused the factory to be struck off Bomber Command's target list for fear of killing French civilians – the factory worked night shifts as well as day. Cheshire was certain that nearby homes would not be hit if his squadron could place their bombs in the right place. In order to clear the factory of workers, the pilots were to fly several runs over the factory before actually dropping their bombs. On this occasion it was decided to use movie film to cover the operation. Pat Moyna, who had flown for his unit on operations to Essen, Hamburg, Bremen and Krefeld, frequently returning in shot-up aircraft, was to be the cameraman. He had his 35mm movie camera fitted in the chosen Lancaster, by cutting away half the side door and using two huge mirrors to reflect as much as possible. 617 would do their own target marking.

By the time the attack was mounted, information was received that the factory was now making engines for the huge German aircraft the Messerschmitt 323, and that in January 1944 it had produced some 115 motors. Just as important was the news that the factory now employed a little over 2,000 people.

Cheshire and Martin, leader and deputy leader, took off fifteen minutes before the main force in order to find and mark the target before they arrived, so as to prevent them circling while they did so. The cloud, as forecast, was between 5,000 and 6,000 feet. It was not thick enough to obscure the moon but thick enough to obscure the ground for any aircraft flying above it.

The two leaders flew below this cloud at a height of about 4,000 feet while the main force flew overhead. The target could be clearly seen from this height and after identification, Cheshire called up Martin and told him he would wait ten minutes before marking to make certain the markers would not be extinguished before the others arrived.

At zero minus ten, the cloud broke and the target was completely clear. Cheshire then made three runs over the factory at 100 feet, giving ample time for a warning to be given to the workers and to check his planned run-in. All the lights in the workshops were on, the blackout in the town and factory being very poor. From a height of about 50 feet the markers were dropped in the centre of the factory site by Cheshire, consisting of fourteen 30 lb incendiaries, five spot fires and eight flares. Red Spot Fires were long burning markers which ignited barometrically at 3,000 feet and which burned up to ten minutes after reaching the ground.

Cheshire dropped at 11.53 and Martin followed this up six minutes later, although the actual factory, being in a valley, was obscured while on a low level run until the very last moment. No sooner had the markers gone down than all the factory lights went off while Cheshire called up the main force using the code-word 'Commando' – Markers dead centre. He then climbed to 5,000 feet to watch the bombing.

The first bomb dropped was by Dave Shannon at two minutes past midnight. His 12,000-lb bomb scored a direct hit right in the middle of the markers. This was followed by a stick of 11 x 1,000 lb bombs by Bob Knights which fell across the western edge. Ken Brown, now a flight lieutenant, and Bunny Clayton dropped 12,000-pounders, followed by Nick Knilans with a stick of 1,000-pounders. David Wilson, Kearns, Willsher and Squadron Leader Suggitt all followed, and Ross reported that his bomb went through the roof of the main building; and it was entered in his Log Book as a direct hit.

Both Cheshire and Martin flew down to inspect the damage and for the next twenty minutes a number of low level runs were made over the factory in order to take photographs from the two 35mm cameras which Pat Moyna was operating. This film is now held and can be viewed at the Imperial War Museum in London. Moyna could only get good shots when the Lancaster flew in from the north, but it showed that great damage had been caused to the entire factory and that only the north-western sheds were still standing.

The route home lay from a point north of Poitiers, West to the island of Yeu and from there out to sea round the Brest peninsula. Most important was that everyone returned safely to complete a successful operation.

A letter was sent to the AOC-in-C, Bomber Command, from the Chief of the Air Staff, Sir Charles Portal, which read:

I have seen the photographs of the Gnôme and Rhône Aero-engine Factory at Limoges taken after the attack on 8/9th February by 617 Squadron. The very severe damage by so small a number of aircraft is most remarkable and I should be grateful if you would convey my warmest congratulations to the squadron on the extreme accuracy of their bombing.

The official damage report showed that 50% of the factory had been destroyed. Out of 48 bays, 21 were destroyed, three severely damaged and 17 more suffered roof damage. The casualties at the factory were slight, only five wounded, two seriously. Much of the credit for this successful attack had to go to Squadron Leader Richardson, known to everyone as 'Talking Bomb'. Don Richardson had joined 617 in August 1943 from No 1 Air Armament School where he was recognised as one of the leading air bombing instructors in the RAF. His main job had been to convert the squadron onto the SABS – the Stabilising Automatic Bomb Sight, a sight which incorporated a gyro.

In perfect conditions bomb aiming could be quite accurate when a SABS was used correctly. One drawback was that it was a little complicated to operate and the Lancaster carrying it needed at least a straight and level run-in of ten miles to the target. Bomber Harris felt his crews had enough problems without a long bomb run, exposed to both flak and fighters. Cochrane could, however, see the advantages of its use, especially against specific or precision targets and won the argument for 617 to use it.

It had been Bob Hay who had christened Richardson 'Talking Bomb', for he seemed to talk of nothing else from dawn till dusk. A pilot from WW1, Richardson eventually flew with 617 on eight raids in order to watch his bomb sight in operation and much of the squadron's success in bombing was due to his love and devotion to his 'baby'. He was rewarded with the AFC, having notched up 249 flying hours on both operations and instructional sorties.

Success did not come easily, but over the next few months the ability to bomb more accurately came to bomb aimers and crews, adding yet more prestige to 617's achievements.

It was back to the Anthéor Viaduct on 12th February. Military supplies were still pouring over the viaduct each day, destined for the Italian front. Over recent weeks it had been used to the maximum.

The plan on this occasion was to carry 12,000 lb bombs filled with Torpex, as even with a direct hit it was difficult to cause any real damage. It was also known that because of 617's recent attacks, the viaduct was now defended by twelve heavy AA guns and a number of light guns.

Refuelling at Ford, the ten Lancasters set off at 9.45 p.m., headed by Wing Commander Cheshire and Mick Martin (in the middle of an air raid warning), climbing through heavy ice conditions. On arrival at the target Cheshire and Martin, twenty minutes ahead of the others, found conditions so black it was impossible to see the viaduct when flying above 3,000 feet. Both men tried repeatedly to carry out a bombing run and were engaged by guns and searchlights. At two minutes before zero hour, Martin finally succeeded in making a run while Cheshire flew in to keep the defences occupied. However, Martin was then subjected to heavy AA fire. Hits registered on his Lancaster and the veteran bomb-aimer Bob Hay was hit and killed. The damage had been caused by a 20mm cannon on the bridge itself and its fire killed Hay as he was in the act of releasing the markers, so close to the point that Martin thought his markers had gone down. Escaping the area, followed by intense flak, other members of the crew went forward to find Hay dead and Ivan Whittaker, the engineer, wounded in the legs. The aircraft was severely damaged and Martin had no choice but to head for and land in Sardinia, now in American hands. Here they buried Bob Hay and put Whittaker into hospital.

As the main formation arrived, Nick Knilans saw Martin's bomber surrounded by flak and his own gunner, Roy Learmouth, took shots at the searchlights. At 1.23 a.m., Cheshire, despite flak damage to his Lancaster, managed to drop eight spot fires, two TIs and 32 x 30 lb incendiaries from 7,000 feet. The red spot fires eventually fell onto the nearby beach. Only one bomb got within fifteen yards of the viaduct and others no nearer than eighty yards. Cheshire attempted another run but was too heavily engaged and had to break off. At 1.35 the force was instructed to return to base, leaving the viaduct still standing, which must have been galling for not just the crews but for two men who flew down to Ford with them, Group Captain Johnson, Woodhall's Station Commander, and Squadron Leader T.W. Lloyd, DSO, the Station IO[1], an old soldier from WW1 who had joined the RAF when WW2 began.

The Lancasters left Ford the next morning to return to Woodall Spa. At about 8.30 a.m., Squadron Leader Bill Suggitt reduced height, came through low clouds and hit the ground at Littleton Down, which at 836 feet above sea level was the highest point on the South Downs of Sussex. One of the first people to arrive at the crash was George Scutt,[2] a tractor driver at Duncton Hill Farm. He found wreckage everywhere, the aircraft having hit a tree at the top of the hill which smashed one of the wings, swung it round as it hit the ground where it disintegrated. All the crew except Suggitt died instantly. Suggitt was still strapped in his seat shouting, 'Turn the engines off.' He died two days later without regaining consciousness. One of his crew had been John Pulford, DFM, Gibson's engineer on the Dams Raid.

[1] Intelligence Officer
[2] Later awarded Kings Commendations

37

CHAPTER FIVE

Tallboy

The squadron had been carrying the 12,000 lb Tallboy bomb over recent raids. Designed by Barnes Wallis, the bomb was first tested in February 1943. Its case was of cast steel with three exploders fitted in the tail while the nose was solid, but later made of Bakelite when it was found that the solid-nosed version tended to turn round after hitting the ground, coming to a stop facing upwards. The main consideration when using these bombs was that the bomber crew had but one only, so it needed to be on target – there was no second chance.

Barnes Wallis, of course, was no stranger to 617 Squadron. Indeed, if it had not been for his idea to knock out the Dams, and then design a special bomb with which to do it (Upkeep, or the 'Bouncing Bomb'), 617 Squadron would not have come into existence – at least not in the form it now was. After the Dams Raid the Bouncing Bomb was never used again.

Barnes Wallis, in 1943, was fifty-six years old, and had an impressive string of achievements behind him. Perhaps an even longer string if people in positions of authority had been able to grasp some of his ideas and concepts, which invariably were proved right – sometimes by other people. During the First World War he had been a design engineer and later had invented the Geodetic method of aircraft construction, used in the Wellesley bomber which he designed for Vickers in 1935. Later he was a leading light behind the successful Wellington bomber and later still, its successor the Warwick. Not so well known is that he had been the designer of the R.100, Britain's most successful dirigible, in the 1920's.

Following the Dams Raid, his active mind continued to wrestle with the problems of hitting and destroying German targets of either special construction or targets that were difficult to hit by conventional bombing. With aircraft now capable of carrying heavier bomb loads his mind turned to larger bombs such as the 12,000-pounder, that might destroy targets with one hit.

No 617 Squadron used these bombs again on the night of 2/3rd March against an aircraft factory at Albert, France. Formerly a machine tool factory, it had been taken over for the assembly of aero-engines for Caudron–Renault, the Germans using it for engine repairs – thought to be those of BMW for use in FW190 fighters. Since a damaging attack by Bomber Command in May 1943 it had been camouflaged and the main building covered with netting on which dummy roads had been painted.

Following a wait for the right weather conditions, fifteen aircraft took off for Albert, led by Cheshire, on his 75th operation, with Les Munro as deputy. Despite the weather forecast, they found cloud and icy conditions en route, which caused some navigational problems but the two leaders arrived in the vicinity of Albert to find the target clear of cloud but the ground very dark.

After a ten minute search they located Albert, and Cheshire called for flares from the main force because there was insufficient light to see much ground detail. Cheshire identified the aiming point and pulled round to make his run, but at the crucial moment the bomb sight because u/s. He called Munro to take over, and the New Zealander put down his markers right in the middle of the target just as the last of the flares went out. Seeing the markers on target, Cheshire ordered the others in and with the exception of one bomb which toppled and fell in open country, the rest went down on the factory which was quickly enveloped in smoke and flames.

The factory seemed, to Cheshire, to be in ruins. Certainly it appeared more devastated than Limoges had been. Les Munro said, 'We were called into bomb. This we did, dropping target flares in a run over the target. I dipped my wing and could see the markers go down into the factory area; the bombing was very accurate and it seemed as if all but the second bomb fell on the factory area.'

Group Captain M.G. Philpot, Station Commander at Woodhall, flew with Flying Officer Nicky Ross, and said, 'I was most impressed by the calm way in which Wing Commander Cheshire led the force and gave his orders to the other aircraft all the time.'

There had been sufficient time between the marking and the bombing for French workers in the factory to get to the shelters. The only casualties were six people killed, three of whom were Belgian collaborators who were trying to put out the incendiaries, and three civilians in the streets of Albert who had apparently died from heart failure. The French were impressed by the timing of the attack, and the technique from the point of view of preventing casualties; the raid occurred after work but before bedtime so that people could get to the shelters.

Lieutenant Nick Knilans remembers hearing that after the attack the Germans posted a notice, saying that anyone who turned in a shot-down member of 617 Squadron would be given a reward of £250, as the Gestapo were keen to interrogate someone from the squadron.

Poor weather caused a raid on a German needle-bearing factory at St Etienne on the 4th to be abandoned, although Munro, despite having lost an engine after take-off, carried on to the target area, where cloud prevented the factory being seen except from directly overhead. Cheshire could not drop flares so he flew in low five or six times along a valley until he was able to drop 224 incendiaries down on the western end of the factory. The majority overshot and skidded onto the road just to the west of the factory. At this point the cloud began to thin out making it possible for the rest of 617 to carry out an attack through the gaps. Several bombs hit the target, starting a number of fires. Later photographic reconnaissance showed an area of the factory 170 x 90 yards to be entirely destroyed.

Five days later the target was another important French aero-engine factory this time at Woippyn, near Metz but bad weather over the target called for the attack to be called off. For Flying Officer Duffy (in ME560 'H') it turned out to be an eventful night.

They received the abort signal when they were about twenty minutes from the target, turning for home when they were about thirty miles from Paris. Warrant Officer Evans, in the mid-upper turret, asked permission to leave his position to use the Elsan. To the rest of the crew's amazement, Duffy gave permission, for normally gunners never left their guns while over hostile territory. Just a few moments later, two Ju88 night fighters attacked from astern. Flight Sergeant Tom McLean, the rear gunner, warned the pilot and opened up with a series of long bursts, reporting jubilantly that the leading 88 was going down in flames, but not before the Lancaster was hit. The gunner himself was wounded in one hand and his sight bulb was put out. Meanwhile, the mid-upper had scrambled back into his turret, just in time to see the night fighter crash, also witnessed by the bomb aimer and pilot.

The second 88 now came in, opening fire from the port side at 850 yards. It then came in from the port beam to nearly full astern, firing all the time and closing to 250 yards. Guided by his gunners, Duffy took evasive action, flying the prescribed corkscrew actions while both gunners returned the fighter's fire. They were on target and the 88 was seen to burst into flames and go down by the gunners, bomb aimer and pilot. It was, however, not seen to hit the ground as they were immediately attacked by a single-engined Me109. Both gunners fired as it closed to 600 yards to 450 yards; then after it pulled up under the Lancaster they saw no more of it.

The bomber had several holes in the rear turret and armament chute, and after they had landed at Woodhall and McLean had been taken to hospital, the crew received the congratulations of the AOC, Ralph Cochrane, who had driven down from Group HQ. One of the crew, Don Bell, thought McLean had got all three fighters. It was not the first time that McLean had been in action against night fighters. When with 102 Squadron his Halifax (W7919 'N') had been attacked during a raid on Mannheim on 6th December 1942. Three Ju88s had made attacks, one of which fell in flames. He and the mid-upper then got another which was also seen to go down in flames. It was his eleventh trip and he received an immediate DFM. His CO at that time had been George Holden, later CO of 617.

McLean, a Scot from Paisley went on to complete 39 operations, adding the DFC and Warrant Officer rank to his name. After the war he was told by the International Red Cross that the two probables he had claimed were in fact kills, one being a German ace.[1] With 617, McLean went on to complete a total of 66 ops, remaining in the RAF until 1955.

Nick Knilans also had a scare when returning from the abortive raid on the 15th. On reaching base he was warned that a German intruder was in the vicinity and the flarepath lights were turned off. Despite this he came in and made a safe landing.

The next night, fifteen aircraft were ordered to attack the Cataroux works of the Michelin Tyre factory at Clermont-Ferrand, France, which produced tyres and inner tubes. It worked in conjunction with the Carnes factory just $1\frac{1}{2}$ miles away, the latter dependent on the Cataroux plant for its continued operations. Some 50% of production went to the German army.

It was a no-moon attack, and six aircraft of 106 Squadron, carrying special navigation equipment, would locate the target and drop flares, which would then enable Cheshire to mark the factory. He arrived over the area with three deputy markers, just before 106 arrived, and below they could see the factory lights begin to go out.

The flares, at first, were scattered and a good many off target, but they were eventually concentrated sufficiently to help Cheshire make his run. He had some difficulty in achieving a good run but on the third attempt dropped his three spot fires. However, they fell some 500 yards short, so he instructed his deputies to make runs which were more successful despite flak which hit Munro's aircraft, bursting a tyre.

With the target now well marked, Cheshire ordered the other Lancasters in from the north. There was very little wind and in consequence, a good deal of smoke made subsequent bombing difficult. Nevertheless the bombing was extremely accurate and everyone seemed to put their bomb on the target. One pilot said, 'When I arrived the target area had been perfectly marked out and the bombs were going down right in the centre of it. Fires had already been started and as we made our bombing run I saw one large factory building demolished. Thick smoke was rolling up as we flew away.' The 'Factory Busters', as the new 12,000-pounders

---

[1] Major Heinrich Wohlers, with 29 victories, was killed in action on the night of 15th March 1944, flying with NJG6. He had been awarded the Knight's Cross.

were named, certainly had done their job.

Once again Squadron Leader Moyna was filming the raid from a height of 500 feet but it was difficult as a pall of smoke covered the target. Cheshire sent the following message back to base, 'Michelin's complexion seems a trifle red.' All the aircraft returned safely to base, and Munro once again made a successful landing despite his burst tyre.

A report made in 1945 showed that the blast from the Blockbusters had caused a considerable amount of structural damage; 31% of the building's damage was caused by blast. All production ceased at Cataroux after the attack, although the other plant re-opened in June 1944. Some time after the raid the intelligence boys received a message from the Maquis which stated that after the attack other factory owners in the area became more co-operative in sabotaging their own factories, and that once again notices had been published about turning in any shot-down members of 617.

The pressure on factories was kept up during March, and 617 visited the Poudrerie Nationale factory at Bergerac, which produced explosives and propellant powder, on the 18th. 617 marked up another successful attack, Cheshire sending back the message, 'The powder works would appear to have outlived their usefulness.'

Flight Lieutenant Bunny Clayton was detailed to drop his 12,000-pounder on an armament dump just to the west of the main target. Jim Watson, his bomb aimer, remembers that they also carried a 1,000-lb bomb, which, due to the different terminal velocities of the two bombs, caused the latter to hit first causing the bigger bomb to explode in the air. The direct hits caused a large explosion which destroyed the dump, the flash causing the strike photograph which was taken 30 seconds after the bomb left the aircraft, to be overdeveloped. Explosion flash lasted for 15 seconds and was described as 'fantastic!'

Two days later 617 went for a similar plant at Angoulême, causing considerable damage and destroying several buildings and dumps. Again one aircraft was detailed to go for the explosives dump which blew up successfully. The bomb aimer in this bomber later said, 'After the attack was over we went down to a low level and had a good look at the factory. The whole place was a mass of flames and twisted wreckage.' Air Commodore A.C.H. Sharp AFO, flew as an observer with one of the crews and said, 'This was my twentieth trip and I never thought I should be able to see night precision bombing of such accuracy. The night was so clear all the way across France that we could see lights blinking on the ground.'

'Talking Bomb' Richardson also flew on this operation in Flying Officer Hamilton's aircraft, and once again Cheshire had the attack filmed.

It was back to France again on the 23rd, when 617 attacked the motor vehicle works of the SOC Berliet, situated some four miles south-west of the centre of Lyons. Before the war it had been one of the leading French manufacturers of cars, vans, lorries and railcars, much of which now, went to the German Army. Nearby was the engine works of the SOC Industries Générales des Moteurs d'Aviation. This produced components for aero-engines.

The squadron were once again assisted by 106 Squadron as the Flare Force, but the first flares were dropped too far to the north, so they were instructed to drop more flares further to the south. This time, however, they dropped their flares ten miles too far to the south. Another correction still failed to get on target. Cheshire now had to get his own men to drop their limited supply of flares, which was successful but soon went out. Cheshire flew one marking run just as the flare died, appeared to be on target so ordered the bombing to begin.

On this raid the Lancasters dropped bombs with 100% delay fuses so that Cheshire had to circle the area for half an hour to await the explosions which would tell him if they had been on target. He was rewarded by seeing huge explosions dead in the centre of the factory complex, his message to base reading: 'Cannot guarantee identification but remain hopeful.'

Most of the Lancasters were diverted to Tangmere when fuel began to run low owing to the delays over the target, and only Nick Ross made it back to Woodhall. Owing to Cheshire's even later return to Tangmere, Gerry Hobbs remembers the door of the Nissen hut in which the crews were put opening and Cheshire and the flight commanders coming in to seek vacant beds. They found them all occupied and although they had been fixed up with beds in the Mess, decided that they should share the discomforts of their men. On this occasion their discomfort was assured for they had finally to bed down on some coconut matting on the floor.

When Flight Lieutenant Williams and his crew went out to their aircraft the next morning they were informed that there was an unexploded incendiary shell in one of the fuel tanks, and another had gone through the wing, piercing the tank without exploding.

The attack was unsatisfactory from many points, not the least being the failure of the flare force to light up the correct area. As there were several factories in the vicinity they could not be certain that they had bombed the right one. As the target itself was only detailed shortly before the raid, precise planning had not been possible. One conclusion was that marking of so small a target could only be done from low level or under perfect moonlight conditions from medium height. Cheshire set about finding a solution to the former problem.

CHAPTER SIX

Aircraft Factories

In consequence of the poor results obtained it was decided to pay a return visit to the aero-factory at Lyons on 25th March. This time, Cheshire was given full permission to attack from low level if he thought fit. Also, they were going to use 100% incendiaries.

In view of the bad flare arrangements over recent raids, Flight Lieutenant Kearns was appointed Flare Leader and to him was delegated the entire job of co-ordinating and regulating flare illumination.

For all this the first flares sent down were once again off target but Kearns succeeded in concentrating them over the top within a very short time. Cheshire then went down and made a low level marking run, coming in over the River Rhône. As the factory came into his sights, the second deputy leader, Squadron Leader McCarthy, came in from the opposite side without warning and dropped his entire load of incendiaries. They fell across a factory, some seen burning on the top of a saw-toothed roof exactly like the one known to be part of the target. Cheshire dropped his markers on top of these but then he realised that in fact they had both dropped three or four hundred yards short of the actual target.

Cheshire quickly radioed his deputy leader, gave him an exact bearing and distance from the markers and he flew down to drop his markers. These overshot 50 to 100 yards leaving them more or less in between the first markers and the target. McCarthy came in again to drop his last two spot fires which were dead on target and could be seen burning inside the main shed. Cheshire ordered 617 in to bomb the spot fires but all the bombs fell on the initial markers some four hundred yards to the west of the target, and in spite of some shouting of orders over the air, the bombs continued to fall on the wrong place. Only Flying Officer Ross succeeded in putting one stick of incendiaries in the target area which seemed to start some fires.

Cheshire's message back was only, 'Regret limited damage only.'

In order to overcome the low marking problems, Cheshire had been hinting to Cochrane for some time that this might improve if he could get hold of a couple of twin-engined Mosquito aircraft. With these, he argued, he could mark from a very low level and far more accurately than with a Lancaster. Finally on the 27th March, two Mosquitos were taken on strength. Cheshire went to Colley Grange to collect one and have some flight instruction on the 30th. Within one hour he had mastered it. However, he had to await Cochrane's orders to use them.

Meanwhile, on the 29th, it was back to Lyons. Clear orders were given not to attack from low level, and 106 Squadron were given only flares to drop. Over the target, despite Kearns' efforts, the flare dropping was worse than ever, partly due to the initial flares, which were to act as a guide, failing to ignite. As a result the rest of 106 were at a loss to know what to do.

After fifteen minutes, Kearns ordered 617 aircraft to drop such flares as they had in reserve and these were extremely well concentrated and placed right over the target. Cheshire immediately began his marking run so as to see the target before the flares died away. His markers fell 60 yards to the east of the target centre and the subsequent bombing was very accurate, no bombs falling outside the target area. When the fifteen aircraft turned for home, the factory was burning with great vigour. Cheshire sent the message, 'All bombs within the white apron', which referred to an order from Cochrane that all bombs were expected to fall within a white square marked on the target map. Only two aircraft were hit, Kearns' damaged by heavy flak, and Duffy's which came back on three engines.

Another operation to France came on 5th April; this time it was the aircraft repair plant of Ateliers Regionnaux d'Artillerie de l'Air, at Toulouse, situated in one corner of the Blagna airfield near the River Garonne. For this operation, Cochrane gave permission for the Mosquito to be used, and with Cheshire at its controls, it headed south to mark for seventeen Lancasters of 617, while 148 aircraft from 5 Group attacked other targets in the Toulouse area. 617 carried 8,000 lb AMTX blast bombs while three other Lancaster squadrons were to then attack the same aiming point in the hope of destroying all surrounding buildings.

There was some question as to the distance the Mosquito had to fly and whether it would be able to complete the round trip. John de Havilland himself came to Woodhall Spa that morning and came to the conclusion that without long range tanks the distance was too far. However, Cheshire decided to give it a try, and set off at 6.30 p.m. with Flight Lieutenant Pat Kelly as his navigator.[1]

They arrived over the target six minutes late to find the conditions clear and Cheshire found no difficulty in identifying the aiming point and immediately made his marking run. There was considerable flak, both heavy and light, but none was particularly accurate. It took three runs to satisfy Cheshire that he was on target, and he released four markers at seventeen minutes past midnight. They fell directly into the centre of the target and he then ordered his deputy leader to back up with further markers and for the rest of the squadron to start bombing.

Unfortunately, one of the targets allotted to the rest of the group was marked with similar red TI's and these diverted three of the squadron crews. Apart from this the bombing was exceptionally accurate and the target hit fair and square. After twenty minutes Cheshire's petrol state forced him to set course for home, leaving the target badly damaged either by direct hits or blast. Back home Woodhall was covered in cloud and rain so the aircraft were diverted to RAF Westcott.

Toulouse was the final trip of his tour for Sergeant Ron Pooley, rear gunner to Flight Lieutenant Edward. When Cheshire asked him if he wanted to carry on or take a rest, Pooley felt his luck was running out and that he had used all of his nine lives, so with flight engineer Bobbie McCullough, left 617. He was later posted to India and did a tour on Liberators with 355 Squadron.

There were a number of recommendations for awards in the first part of April, one rather unusual one being the Soviet Medal of Valour to Flying Officer Chandler, DFC, the only one awarded to a

[1] Later Squadron Leader, killed November 1944.

member of 617. Other awards went to Wing Commander Cheshire, a second bar to his DSO, the DSO to Les Munro, bars to DFC to Joe McCarthy and Keith Astbury (Cheshire's bomb aimer) and DFCs for Tammy Simpson, DFM, Watson – after 41 ops, Buttle – after 43 ops, Warrant Officer Dacey – after 53 ops, and Flying Officer Willsher after 31 operations. Warrant Officer Bickley received the Conspicuous Gallantry Medal after no less than 71 ops. Bickley had enlisted in the RAF in 1936, became a corporal in 1939 and a sergeant the following year. He had previously flown with 613 and 44 Squadrons before joining 617 in November 1943. He left them on 18th May 1944.

The target for 10th April was the St Cyr Field Air Park and Signals Equipment Depot, situated 2½ miles north-west of Versailles. Eighteen Lancasters were bombed up, plus Cheshire and Kelly in the Mosquito. On this operations some flyers of the American Air Corps were taken along as observers.

Cheshire marked the target, which stored various kinds of aircraft and aero-engines, which was virtually next door to the famous St Cyr Military College of France. The bombs went down from 8,000 feet, several fires were started and three long buildings were destroyed.

A similar force of 617 flew to the marshalling yards at Juvisy on the 18th, situated on the west bank of the Seine between the River Orge and Orly airfield. The target was important as a control and distribution centre for Paris and the south-west and south-east regions of France. Two veteran Bomber Command squadrons, 83 and 97 – experts in navigation – flew with them to illuminate the target area while Cheshire marked the yards. The attack was made in two waves, the first attacking the southern sector, the other the northern sector, but in order to eliminate the possibility of confusion and the danger of the target becoming obscured by smoke, the two attacks were one hour apart.

Cheshire lost his DR compass en-route and found some difficulty in telling in which direction he was flying, and in consequence found it difficult to locate the aiming point. Finally he let his markers go at 11.21 p.m., judged them to be on target and ordered his third deputy leader in to back up. These too fell on target and 617 came in to bomb. The flares had been dropped successfully although some were scattered, many falling in the centre of Paris, clearly illuminating the Arc de Triomphe, but in the main the yards were illuminated for seven to eight minutes.

Dave Shannon led the second wave and he was able to mark the target beyond any shadow of doubt. One Main Force squadron commander said, 'It was one of the finest examples of precision bombing I have ever seen. It was obvious that all our fellows were taking the most extreme pains to carry out instructions. They had been told how careful they must be to get their bombs among the closely packed target indicators.'

This was the first operation with 617 for Flight Lieutenant Bill Reid, VC. He had previously flown with 61 Squadron and won the Victoria Cross for an operation on 3/4th November 1943 against Düsseldorf. Thirty miles inside the Dutch coast on the outward journey his Lancaster (LM360 'O') was attacked by a Me110 night-fighter, and a few minutes later by a FW190. Despite extensive damage to the aircraft, his navigator being killed, the wireless operator fatally wounded and engineer having a broken arm and himself wounded in the head, arms, hands and shoulder, and then showered with broken glass and perspex as the windscreen was smashed, Reid carried on to the target and bombed it. He then flew home to belly-land when his wheels collapsed as he touched down. He recovered to fly again, this time with 617 Squadron, bringing two of his former crew with him.

It was marshalling yards again on the 20th, this time at La Chappelle near Paris and now 617 had increased its complement of Mosquitos to four and all were used as marker aircraft on this raid. With the invasion of Europe coming up, disruption of German supply routes and its railways system in particular was important – important enough for 617 to be assigned these targets for total destruction in the weeks before D-Day.

The four marker aircraft dropped red spot fires from 5,000 feet down to 200 feet in the case of Cheshire, and the Lancasters planted 168 1,000 lb bombs mainly onto the southern side of the yards.

Two days later, with an operation to Brunswick, 617 was able to use its new marker technique on a target in Germany. 617 formed part of a force of two hundred aircraft which went to Brunswick that night. The raid was only partly successful as some of the flares fell some distance from the target. As it was, 40% of the force aimed at this while 60% aimed at the correct marker. Many of the aircraft carried incendiaries as well as 2,000 lb bombs but some damage was caused to two marshalling yards, railways workshops and sidings. It was in the process of being considerably extended.

The German railway centre at Munich was the next target, on the night of 24th April. With the exception of the Nürnberg Passau line and the Arlberg, all lines from eastern France and south-west Germany to Austria passed through Munich, so too did a large part of the traffic to and from Italy to north and north-west Germany.

It was a large operation, the route being around the southern and eastern boundary of Switzerland while another force was sent to Karlsruhe which subsequently distracted the night-fighters. There was also a diversion over the North Sea – minelaying – and six Lancasters of 617 were sent to Milan as a 'spoof' raid, for they only dropped TIs and flares while red TI route markers were dropped over Lake Annecy.

Illumination was provided by 83 and 97 Squadrons, while 617 carried out the marking and backing up of the aiming points. Cheshire was still trying to get long-range tanks for his Mosquito aircraft but as they were still not forthcoming, they had to refuel and fly out from aerodromes on the English coast – on this night from Manston, which left them with about 15-20 minutes' fuel margin. This meant no dallying over the target.

The main force took off in daylight, climbed above the cloud and set course on their long journey across France, over the Alps into Italy and the north towards Munich. Nearly two hours later, at 11.50 p.m., the Mosquitos took off from Manston climbed to 14,000 feet in order to make use of a strong tail wind and set off in pursuit of the 'heavies'. Just short of the Rhine. while flying through thick thundery cloud, Cheshire called up the deputy for a weather check. He was immediately answered by Mick Martin who by chance was somewhere in the area pursuing his own objective. Martin, having left 617 earlier in the year, was flying with 515 Squadron, a Mosquito night intruder unit; his target this night was German airfields around Bonn.

A few moments later the weather began to clear sufficiently to see

51

the main force attack on Karlsruhe which was well under way. At zero hour they arrived at the datum point, ten miles short of the target and turned for the aiming point together and according to plan. The town was heavily defended by guns and a vast number of searchlights. As they went in they could see the Lancasters way up above illuminated in the cones but ploughing steadfastly through the thick concentration of flak.

As Cheshire reached the target the first flares ignited, an accurate, compact bunch directly over the aiming point. He immediately radioed to say he was running in to mark, put his nose down and dropped two red spot fires at exactly 1.44 a.m. from a 12,000 to 3,000 feet dive at 480 mph. As far as he could see they were directly on target and in consequence 617 was ordered to back up then the main force started to bomb. The three deputy leaders made runs, Shannon and Kearns scoring two further direct hits from a low level altitude, but Flight Lieutenant Fawke's marking failed when all his spot fires hung up.

Immediately after dropping their markers, all four Mosquitos were heavily and accurately engaged by the defences but with a keen eye on their fuel gauges they were compelled to abandon any further part in the attack and made tracks for home. They all landed safely at Manston. As Cheshire landed at 4.22 he had a bout of further drama. When making his approach he was down to just fifteen minutes of fuel, only to be told that an enemy intruder was circling the field. The landing field lights went out and Cheshire told Pat Kelly to turn off their navigation lights, but in the haste to do so he turned off the whole electrical system in the aircraft (they were all in a row on the starboard side), so they came in to land with no lights anywhere. Cheshire asked flying control at Manston to switch on the runway lights and then turn them off as soon as his wheels hit the runway. This was the only time Cheshire remembers Kelly losing his composure; he was cursing and swearing over the flak and the shortage of petrol. When Fawke arrived back he was actually fired upon by the German intruder but he was not hit and landed safely.

One 617 Squadron aircraft was missing after the attack, out of the total of nine Lancasters lost that night. This was Flight Lieutenant J.L. Cooper who was shot down at Aichstetten, en route to Munich. All the crew were taken prisoner except Flying Officer George Harden, the bomb aimer, who was killed. The 'spoof' attack on Milan led by Flight Lieutenant Edward was an unqualified success and very ably executed, although all were unhappy that they were not permitted to drop bombs.

Immediately on landing the entire squadron was given one week's leave by the C-in-C and during this time a complete overhaul of all aircraft was made. Then on 1st May the question of low level marking and the implications based on 617 Squadron's teachings was discussed at Bomber Command Headquarters. The Americans were very interested in this and proposals were put to the Chief of the Air Staff suggesting that the nucleus of a force should be formed to study and train in low level techniques. Cheshire was also asked, unofficially, if he would, together with a small British staff, be prepared to undertake the organisation and training of such a force, should the American Chief of Staff agree to one being formed. Cheshire replied that a number of RAF officers had trained in the techniques, although the number was limited. He suggested either Squadron Leaders Martin or Munro or Flight Lieutenant Rumbles. However eventually the idea was dropped by the powers-that-be.

It was back to the war on 3rd May, when the military barracks at Mailly-Le-Camp was the target. It was eighty miles east of Paris and forty miles south of Rheims. Here the Germans had built up a training and reinforcement camp of front line Panzer units; it housed some 10,000 men as well as elements of the 21st Panzer Division. It was also the main training camp in France for German ammunition units. With the invasion of France only a month away, it was an important target. 300 Lancasters of Bomber Command flew on the raid but 617's only part was for its four Mosquitos to mark the target. Permission was refused for its Lancasters.

The plan was hurried, the order for the attack not being received until late in the day. It would take part in two waves, the first at one minute past midnight, when all good soldiers should be back in barracks, the second eighteen minutes later.

The first two Mossies, piloted by Cheshire and Shannon, were off just after 11 p.m., Kearns and Fawke around twenty minutes later. Navigation proved no problem and the aiming point identified on time. As Cheshire arrived either minutes early he circled a nearby aerodrome pretending to be an intruder; then 83 and 97 Squadrons arrived over the target to drop flares. At midnight Cheshire dived on the camp, dropped his markers and was then backed up by Shannon. The order was then given for the main force to attack but poor communications caused a delay of five minutes; nevertheless the bombing proved accurate and concentrated. The two other Mosquitos went to the west end of the camp and marked the aiming point, Gerry Fawke in a dive to 2,000 feet, Terry Kearns from 3,000 feet. Shortly before this Cheshire told the force controller to cease bombing but this did not happen. Cheshire then ordered the controller to send in the second wave to bomb the existing markers but this was not passed on, so in view of the fierce air battle which had developed overhead he ordered the second and third deputies to remark the aiming point despite the falling bombs. When this was done the controller sent in the second wave although the new markers were hardly to be seen through the smoke. This delay led to aircraft of the second wave circling the area for an inordinate time and was a direct cause of the subsequent heavy losses sustained from enemy night fighter attacks. In all 46 aircraft, nearly all from the second wave, failed to get home. In marking the target on the second time, the 617 markers showed great courage, being engaged by light flak the whole time. In addition, Cheshire and Shannon dive-bombed light flak posts and they stopped firing, but whether they had been hit or just stopped was hard to know.

Despite fighter attack, 1,500 tons of bombs were dropped killing 218 soldiers and wounding 156 more. 114 barrack blocks, 47 training huts and some ammunition stores were hit, while 102 vehicles, including 37 tanks, were destroyed. In the air battle a number of night fighters were shot down.

There was some criticism of Cheshire and his team of markers but the main cause of the poor results and high losses was the failure in communications with the master controller. Next day his radio was found to be 30 kilocycles off frequency, which caused the signal to be very weak and difficult to receive.

*

During off duty periods, 617's cricket team played matches against teams from Boston, Skegness, Gainsborough, etc. They had several good Australian players in the team, such as Ross Stanford who had played for South Australia before the war. He had also played for the Australian Services Team at Lords. He and Jim Heveron, the Orderly Room Sergeant, put on 150 runs against Gainsborough one weekend, the same weekend Stanford knocked up 100 at Lords. Other members of 617's team were Arthur Kell, Maxie Tuxford, Mike Vaughan and Bill Gover, who came from Lincolnshire was team Captain. They later won the 5 Group Knockout Cup, beating RAF Coningsby in the final.

On 16th May the squadron held a party to celebrate the first anniversary of the Dams Raid. Guy Gibson was unable to attend but many of the surviving participants did as well as people from A.V. Roe and Vickers who did so much towards the success of the raid.

Three days later came a dance to further celebrate the raid for all ranks. This time Gibson did attend and was given a rousing reception by everyone. A special cake was made and both Gibson and Cheshire made speeches. For this they stood on a table but Gibson slipped and put his leg in the cake, quickly making a remark about 'icing' – the aircrew nightmare. By all accounts it was a wild party and the beer flowed like water.

It was a fitting end for several of the original 617 boys who were being posted away, such as Toby Foxlee, Tammy Simpson, Danny Walker, Ken Brown, Ivan Whittaker, Clay Johnson and Goodale who had all flown in the raid that made 617 so famous.

CHAPTER SEVEN

D-Day

Planning for the D-Day operation began in December 1943 and had the original code name 'Bigotted'. Dr Robert Cockburn was taken to the planners' map room at Norfolk House and shown a map of Normandy with all the possible landing positions and was asked to produce a 'spoof' invasion force as a diversion to the main landings. During January and February 1944 he investigated the possibility of dropping controlled 'window'[1] against ground radar, supported by a seaborne moonglow device against airborne radar. Trials were carried out against captured German radar in late March 1944 and early April at Toutallou on the Firth of Forth in Scotland. This Moonglow equipment was installed in air sea rescue launches operated by a US Army signal detachment from Iceland.

Early in May tactical exercises began off Flamboro Head on the Yorkshire coast. The crews were not sure what it was all about at the time, which was nothing new for 617, but it required high precision, flying one minute legs. In between, time was spent in endless counting of 'window' strips and packing them in exact numbered bundles. The squadron was split into two halves, and while one would fly, the other would watch the radar screens, to see the effect of the 'window' being dropped.

On the 13th a full scale trial was carried out by 617 at Bempton ground station (near Flamboro Head) against one of Britain's radar stations. Cheshire flew a Lancaster at about 100 feet all the way. Dr Cockburn, who was on board, remembered it being a 'very hairy trip', as he sat wondering if they would clear the low lying

---

[1] 'Window' was the code name for bundles of aluminium strips, dropped from aircraft to confuse German radar.

power cables. The whole of May was taken up with this training[1], and while in Yorkshire, many of the crews spent some of their spare time scaling cliffs looking for seagulls' eggs which were brought back for tea.

It was found that an illusion of a mass of shipping could be produced on ship-watching radar with the use of 'window' along paths spaced two miles apart, provided the height of release was less than 3,000 feet, the size of the bundles being increased as the coast was approached and the 'window' replenished every seven minutes. The scheme was given the code word 'Taxable' and in using it, it was hoped to fool the Germans into thinking an invasion force was approaching the Calais area, rather than Normandy.

The aircraft trained to fly in boxes of four flying straight tracks four miles apart and about eight miles along a Gee lattice line towards the hostile coast. An accurate rate one turn, through 180° onto a course parallel to and two miles from the inward course, finally completed the orbit with a rate one turn within seven minutes. One box of four would patrol on the length 30-38 miles from the coast, the second 38-46 miles away, the first flying at 3,000 feet, the second, 2,500, each dropping 'window' at a rate of 36 bundles during each leg of every orbit. This then appeared on the radar screens as ships heading for France at a speed of eight knots.

On the night of 5th June, while the actual invasion force headed towards the Normandy beaches, 617 Squadron flew at 160 mph, keeping the correct height by radio altimeter, and making their turns according to a navigator's stop-watch. The 'spoof' force was pretending to be making for a spot near Cap d'Antifer, east of Le Havre.

Len Sumpter of Dave Shannon's crew remembers two men at the chute, one pushing out 'window' while the other held a stop-watch to ensure the bundles going out every 15 seconds. On the first run the bundles were very thin but as each leg was completed so the size of the bundles increased. Each aircraft carried two pilots, each taking turn to fly the legs. To some crews it seemed an anti-climax, no target, no bombs, and when they flew back in the early morning light they could see the vast invasion force below them on its way to

[1] This was the reason Lancasters could not be used for the raid on Mailly.

the greatest invasion ever seen. Gerry Witherick, flying with Flying Officer Willsher said, 'If you had baled out you would have not have got your feet wet as the sea was covered with ships, from England to France.'

At dawn a flotilla of E-boats were seen some way off and Flying Officer Duffy's gunners opened fire on them. Later he suffered a 'strip' being torn off him for risking their cover being blown. They were also shelled by shore batteries on the French coast.

Leonard Cheshire remembers it as a long operation, calling for a high degree of precision flying. Yet the 'spoof' was very successful, for it kept German forces on the alert in the Pas de Calais area, where they remained until it was too late for them to help repel the real invasion. 218 Squadron was also involved in this operation; their code name was 'Glimmer' and they operated off Boulogne.

Wing Commander Cheshire felt the air crews needed some form of escape and evasion training at this time, so one day he put them on a bus or two, without their caps, wallets and money, and with the windows blacked out driven 15-20 miles out into the country. When dropped off, they were told to get back to base, the control tower at Woodhall being the finishing point, and that local police and Home Guard units had been alerted.

Soon after Nick Knilans and his crew were dropped, a car came along and as luck would have it it was driven by an old friend from 9 Squadron. He gave them a lift into Boston where they stayed in the White Hart pub till ten, then borrowed some money from the bar maids for the bus fare back to Woodhall, where they entered the station by a back entrance. They never did receive the bottle of whisky promised to every man who got back undetected!

On the actual day of the invasion, Les Munro took his T-Tommy (EE145) up for an air test and short low level cross country exercise. Percy Pigeon, his wireless operator, found there were 'gremlins' in the VHF radio. While they were away from base it rained and as Munro came in to land he found someone else coming in to land on the same track. He decided to go ahead and land parallel, with the other Lancaster to port of him. This entailed coming over the bomb dump and shortening his length of available runway by 300 yards. With this in his mind, Munro put on the brakes as soon as he hit the runway. No sooner had he done so than the grass, being wet, caused the wheels to lock and the aircraft started to skid to the left. The strain caused the undercarriage to collapse and the Lancaster shot along the runway on its belly, bending the four propellers in the process. They finished up across a small road, but still inside the airfield boundary. The gunners, Harry Weeks and Bill Howarth, had to rotate their turrets by hand to line them up to enable them to get out. They were all taken to sick quarters but none was hurt. For this landing, Les Munro was given an endorsement in his log book and although he got his leg pulled for some weeks afterwards, the general opinion was that he had been very harshly treated.

The Tallboy bomb had now been developed so as to achieve a deep penetration of the earth and thereby to cause damage to underground workings and tunnels by ground shock. The casing was made of special chrome molybdenum steel, filled with Torpex D1, the charge weight being 5,000 lbs, with an overall length of 21 feet. On 8th June, 617 took them to the South of France to use against the Saumur railway tunnel and bridge. Its destruction would stop the flow of German reinforcements from south-west France to the Normandy invasion area.

Three Mosquitos and twenty-one Lancasters took part, each Tallboy having 25-second time fuses, and the flare force was provided by ten Lancasters from 83 Squadron. Soon after take-off, Shannon had to return with an engine problem but Cheshire and Fawke reached the target shortly after 2 am, Cheshire putting down his markers from 500 feet, Fawke dropping his thirty minutes later on the north end of the tunnel, which fell only fifty yards off target.

To most of the crews the bombing seemed concentrated, at least two direct hits seen on the markers. Flying Officer Sanders, in P-Popsie (ED909) Mick Martin's old Dams aircraft which had the bomb bay cut away to accommodate the Tallboy bomb, observed several bombs straddle the bridge just like a 'stick of bombs'. One fell on the roof of the tunnel thirty yards from the entrance which caused it to collapse. Hits were also scored on the edge of the cutting 50 yards from the tunnel entrance causing the side of the cutting to slide down over the tracks. Later it was known that 10,000 tons of earth collapsed into the tunnel, the Germans being unable to clear it before the area was liberated in August 1944.

German E-boats, using the harbours of Le Havre and Boulogne, had for years been attacking shipping in the Channel but now they were an even bigger danger to the convoys supporting the invasion front. On 14th June 617 were briefed to attack their pens at Le Havre with their Tallboy bombs hoping the earthquake effects underwater would create a tidal wave which would smash the E-Boats against the docks and concrete pillars.

Twenty-two Lancasters, led by Munro, and with three Mosquitos, took off at 8.15 p.m. with a fighter escort of Spitfires. As they were flying towards the Channel an Australian voice came over the air, nattering to his crew. It came from a recce aircraft of 463 Squadron and, the pilot was giving speed details of, height and other important facts, which may well have been picked up by the Germans. It made the Lancaster crews a little nervous as they approached the French coast, where they were met with heavy flak. Several aircraft were hit and a few turned back on three engines. The rest carried on as the sky darkened and the Spitfires left them.

Cheshire dived down to 7,000 feet to drop his markers, being surrounded by exploding AA shells, followed by Shannon and Fawke. Les Munro led in the Lancasters, his bomb falling dead on the aiming point and he also saw two other bombs make direct hits, one of whose was Knilans' bomb. Knilans' bomb aimer saw many Tallboys splash into the harbour water, causing large explosions. Their mid-upper gunner Sergeant Alf 'Bing' Crosby, however, was wounded when light flak exploded around their aircraft, but he stayed in his turret till they reached home. On landing he was taken to hospital where his leg wound festered, keeping him in bed for two weeks.

On this operation, Pilot Officer Jimmy Castagnola, who was destined for fame with 617, flew as a passenger. He felt it was better than staying back at base waiting for the boys to return.

No 460 Squadron, also on this raid, dropped 1,000 lb and 4,000 lb Blockbusters, but one load nearly came down on the aircraft of Flight Lieutenant Poore (in DV391 'O'), but he put his Lancaster into a steep turn and avoided the falling bombs.

A follow-up attack was carried out some two hours later and when a photo-recce was flown the next day, the photographs appeared to show that most of the E-Boats had been sunk. Some torpedo boats at the side of the deep-water quay near the passenger railway station, and at the end of the north quay, were also sunk. One of these was burning when the first photos were taken but it had sunk by the time the aeroplane left. Another boat could be seen lying in a damaged condition on a bank close to the east wall of the pens. The pens themselves had been hit and damage caused to the roof. A large floating dock had been sunk and tremendous damage done to quayside buildings.

With the success at Le Havre, 617 were assigned to attack Boulogne the next night whilst other units of Bomber Command bombed nearby harbour installations. The actual E-Boat pens lay between Basin Loubet and Avant-Port and, like Le Havre's pens, they too were of reinforced concrete, with roofs 10 to 11 feet thick. The six shelters housed about fourteen boats.

Thick clouds began over the Channel, reaching a height of about 13,000 feet. When the harbour was reached, heavy flak met the Lancasters, but because of the weather ten of the twenty-two Lancasters brought their bomb back. Cheshire marked the target with two red spot fires, plus two 500-lb MCs, at 11.45 p.m., from 6,000 feet. The remaining twelve Lancasters of 617 descended below the clouds to bomb from between 7,000 and 13,000 feet. Once again an Australian voice came over the air; Arthur Kell was blamed but was later vindicated and blame put on a recce crew in the vicinity.

Les Munro led them in but flak hit several aircraft, including McCarthy's, Kearns', Clayton's, Howard's, Poore',s Knight's and Stout's. Flying Officer Duck, bomb aimer to Flying Officer Hamilton, was wounded in the thigh and his aircraft hit at least three times in the petrol tanks. He also had one of his bomb doors blown off but carried on to bomb. Landing at Manston, Duck had twenty-seven pieces of shrapnel taken out of his leg.

The cloud layer spoilt the attack, many crews being unable to identify the target. Nick Knilans had a narrow escape as he finished his bomb run. He heard, 'Look up, Nicky!' from Jimmy Castagnola. He did so and saw a dozen 1,000-pounders coming at him out of the darkness. Another Lancaster had just dumped its bomb load down through the clouds. He made a steep diving turn to port and his rear gunner, Roy Learmouth claimed he could have patted one of the bombs as it hurtled past his turret.

Despite all this, later recce photos showed that over 130 E-boats had been destroyed. Some of the Tallboys had gone through the roofs of the pens and destroyed boats there. In addition thirteen vessels in the harbour were wrecked or badly damaged and oil storage tanks burnt out.

CHAPTER EIGHT

V-Weapon Sites

On 29th June 1943 the War Cabinet Defence Committee met to discuss the latest findings of the Duncan Sandys investigations into the probability that the Germans were working on a secret weapon, thought then likely to be a long range rocket. It was not known at that stage that there were in fact three V-weapons, as they became known: the V1 (flying bomb); the V2 rocket; and the V3, the long range gun which fortunately never became operational against Britain. One immediate step after the Committee meeting was to put in hand orders for the now famous raid on the German experimental rocket base at Peenemünde in August 1943, which was being used for the development of both the rocket and the flying bomb. This caused a delay in the rocket programme, but by early 1944 it was obvious that the threat was still a very real one. In addition, the smaller V1 flying bomb whose existence was by now known would soon be ready for use against Britain from the so-called ski sites that had been springing up all over Northern France.

The sites attacked by 617 were of two categories: the smaller ski-sites bombed during the early part of 1944, and the so-called 'large sites' intended both for storage and for underground launching. The most ominous large sites were at Watten in the Pas de Calais, and at Wizernes, both of which it was later discovered had been intended for the storage and firing of the V2 rocket. Watten had first been successfully attacked by Bomber Command in August 1943, and as a result its use had been changed and Wizernes designated instead for use by the V2. But in 1944 construction began again at Watten, and thus it once more became a prime target. The first attack by 617 Squadron was made on Watten on

19th June 1944, four days after the first flying bombs had landed in England. The site was situated on the south-east fringe of the forest of Eperlecque, one mile from Watten and six miles north of St Omer.

Cheshire and Shannon again marked the target with spot fires and 500 lb bombs, but the spot fires failed to ignite so the bomber force had to attack visually, led by Joe McCarthy. Eighteen Tallboys went down, each having 11-second fuses, but cloud over the target covered results. However, Shannon dived down and reported at least five hits only 50 yards from the aiming point.

Knilans bombed from 18,000 feet, keeping the needle of the bomb sight on his instrument panel right on the centre mark. This needle was about 5 x 2 inches and as the bomb aimer on his panel altered the bomb sight this showed on the pilot's panel so that he could adjust the aircraft accordingly. He therefore, applied light rudder and stick corrections to keep the needle steady during the run in to the drop.

'Bombs away,' yelled Taffy Rodgers, as the red light went out on his bomb sight. There was no surge upwards – the bomb had hung up! 'All switches safe,' said Taffy, rather distraught.

'Okay, Taffy, we'll take the damn thing home.' But before the bomb doors were closed, the Tallboy dropped away. Later photographs showed that this bomb made a huge crater 2½ miles south of the target.

Flight Lieutenant Howard also had his bomb hang up, but unlike Knilans his did not drop clear and he flew home with it. Flying Officer Ross also had trouble and had to release his bomb manually; in so doing it overshot by about 150 yards. The result, however, was that the site had been completely knocked out and further thoughts for its use were abandoned. Later inspection of the site in November showed that one Tallboy had hit the top of the main structure, dislodged a huge piece of concrete of some 300 tons which had fallen onto a small concrete out-building.

The second large site target for 617 was at Wizernes. Construction had begun in November 1943, after the partial destruction of Watten, but it had not yet been completed. Situated on the northern face of a hill to the south of the main railway line from St Omer to Boulogne, it was close to Wizernes station. Three

Mossies and nineteen Lancasters headed for it on 20th June, but cloud made it impossible so it was back on the bombing list two days later, this time with only sixteen bombers and the Mosquitos. But again the target was covered with cloud and had to be abandoned.

The third attempt was made on the 24th. Over the target Cheshire was unable to release his markers so it was left for Fawke to drop four smoke bombs as an area marker, but his Mosquito was hit several times by flak. Flak also scored hits on the Lancasters flown by Munro, Stanford, Knight and Poore but bombs rained down on the target and at least two bombs hit the railway line. A launching tunnel had been canted several degrees by one hit.

The flak, however, claimed one victim – Flight Lieutenant Edward and his crew. He was hit over the target in the port wing and seen to go down out of control and explode before hitting the ground. It was 617's first casualty since February and because it was in daylight, everyone could see the bomber go down and know who was in it. They were at 17,500 feet when hit, flying straight and level towards the target. The wireless operator, Gerrard Hobbs, saw the port inner engine on fire and heard the word 'Abracadabra' on the intercom – the code signal to abandon aircraft.

He clapped on his 'chute but while doing so he saw it was spilling out of its pack and tried to prevent more from doing so. He climbed onto the main spar to go aft and jump from the rear door but he met the mid-upper Flying Officer Johnstone, who said there was too much fire at the rear to do so. Suddenly the aircraft began to shudder. Flying Officer Bill King, the flight engineer, was lying on the floor. Hobbs then saw Edward leave his seat and make for the front hatch; it was his intention to follow but owing to lack of oxygen he passed out and knew no more until he came round in a field with German soldiers and some French civilians standing round him. His right arm and leg were both broken and in an adjoining field he saw pieces of smouldering aeroplane.

In jumping from the aircraft, Sergeant Brook lost both flying boots and landed in a poppy field where he was captured by the Germans.

One of the Frenchmen was André Schamp, a farmer from St Omer. He saw the Lancaster hit by gunfire from AA posts in

Mussent. He remembers the guns had several white rings painted on the barrels, each one indicating an aircraft shot down. As the bomber came down Schamp was horrified to see such a large thing falling towards him. He ran first to the left, then to the right, but still the 'plane was above him. Finally at about 100 to 150 metres from the ground it changed direction and exploded, hitting the ground 200 metres away. He went straight to the wreckage in spite of the exploding ammunition. The left wing and cockpit were on fire. He found a man lying on his stomach, turned him over but found he was dead. It was the pilot, John Edward. A second man was Johnstone, the mid-upper. He was still alive but badly wounded and never regained consciousness, dying in St Omer hospital.

Schamp also found Sam Isherwood but he too was beyond help. A fourth man, Gerry Hobbs was sitting in a field with a broken leg and arm. Hobbs gestured to him with his good arm to his top pocket. André Schamp opened it, located the packet of Players cigarettes and lit one for him. Shortly afterwards Hobbs was lifted onto a stretcher, then onto a truck in which hay had been spread to make it more comfortable, and then driven to St Omer hospital.

The next day, at the close of a church service, a German lorry drove up and André Schamp was ordered to empty it. In it were the bodies of Edward and Isherwood. He took both bodies into the church. The body of rear gunner Tom Price was still in the crashed aircraft. Schamp, after three visits to the Germans in Longuenesse, finally obtained permission to collect and bury him. The three men were buried alongside each other, the inscription on their grave reading: 'I will lift up mine eyes unto the hills from whence cometh my help.'

A month later the body of Bill King was found in a field. He had been thrown 200 metres. The unexploded bomb was also located; flat on the ground it had fallen and gone into the earth to a depth of two or three metres. It was removed by prisoners in dark clothing.

Gerry Hobbs awoke in a room on his own. He couldn't feel his right leg but pulling back the sheets found it encased in plaster but his toes were turning black – it was too tight. A doctor came in and looking at Gerry, who had a moustache, joked, 'Mr Anthony Eden!' and laughed. He examined the leg and cut the plaster open, at which time the hospital was strafed by an aircraft. Later that day

66

he was taken to a hospital in Lille where he met up with Jackie Brook and Lorne Pritchard, the bomb aimer and navigator. Hobbs ended up in Stalag IXC where he remained until liberated by Patton's army in 1945.

André Schamp is still living in St Omer and recently told his story to a newspaper, *L'Indépendant du Pas-De-Calais*, published in November 1981. The outcome was a contact with Gerry Hobbs, now living on the Isle of Wight.

Following this attack, 617 were sent against another large site at Siracourt, this one designed for the V1. It was situated on high open ground, ¾ of a mile south of the Hesdin St-Pol-sur-Temoise road. Its discovery was first noted in September 1943 — parallel trenches being observed which were later concreted over to form the extension of the main railway line. The site was capable of launching two flying bombs an hour towards London, 130 miles away. 617 assigned seventeen Lancasters, two Mosquitos plus Wing Commander Cheshire in a newly acquired Mustang fighter!

In his constant search for more accurate ways to put markers down on a target, Cheshire felt that a single-engined fighter would be even better than a Mosquito. He had met the American Generals Spaatz and Doolittle on a few occasions, for the Americans were very interested in 617's bombing techniques and its record, and so it was not too difficult for him to acquire a Mustang. It was a private gift from the American air force and it arrived at Woodhall Spa, in its packing case, on 25th June – the day of the raid on Siracourt. He got the ground crews to assemble it, clean off the protective grease, check over the engine and prepare it for the operation. As the time passed it became obvious that there would be no time for a test flight and indeed the fighter was still not ready when the Lancasters took off. An hour after they had left, Cheshire took a final mouthful of tea from his fitter's mug, then took off – his first flight in not only this Mustang, but any Mustang.

He had now to do his own navigation, but found his way, and with a speed of around 375 mph, quickly caught up the main force. He dived down to 500 feet dropped two red spot fires, followed up by Shannon who put down four smoke bombs and two further spot fires, and Fawke with four smoke bombs.

Les Munro again led in the Lancasters and he himself saw two direct hits on the trenches and Cheshire himself saw a number of direct hits. Flying Officer Lee was shot up by flak but managed a bombing run only to have his bomb hang up on his first run. On a second run it still failed to release so they had finally to jettison it over the sea. Nevertheless, the bombing in total was good and the site knocked out – another success for 617.

As a sidelight, it was about this time that Nicky Knilans decided to buzz the Petwood Hotel, used by 617 as their Officers' Mess. His Lancaster roared over the roof with about three feet to spare and so terrified a WAAF waitress that she dropped an entire tray of tea things over the Station Commander, Group Captain Philpott. It was only the timely intervention by Cheshire that saved the American's bacon on this occasion.

The next target for 617 was a flying bomb storage dump at St Leu d'Esserent, Pas de Calais, in the Creil area, on 4th July. Here the Germans were storing the V1 flying bombs. Before the war the buildings were used by French farmers for growing mushrooms and the roofs were on average, five feet thick.

One Mustang, one Mosquito and seventeen Lancasters headed for France, Cheshire marking the AP at 1.30 p.m. in a dive from 5,000 to 800 feet. His marking was accurate but his VHF system failed. The bombers attacked, and although three crews failed to identify the target, the others bombed well, scoring one direct hit, and a near miss made the entrance useless. The railway line was also completely destroyed. Sir Arthur Harris visited the site after the area had been liberated and on meeting a small boy commented on the awful mess. Asking the boy what the smell was he received the reply, 'There are 800 Boche trapped in there!' One bomb hit had completely sealed the main tunnel and crushed two rockets complete with their war-heads.

Another crew not to bomb was that of Pilot Officer Sanders when his switchgear became u/s. They were then attacked by a Ju88 at a height of 15,000 feet. His mid-upper and rear gunners returned its fire and saw it burst into flames and dive to the ground.

The large sites continued to receive 617's attention, but the next, at Mimoyecques, in the Pas de Calais, was slightly different. Its purpose was to house the V3, the large guns that would fire small, relatively light shells to London – a distance of 95 miles. The shell was estimated to be about six inches in calibre with a weight of about 120 pounds packed with some 40 lbs of high explosives. The enemy might have attained a rate of fire equivalent to a salvo of 25 rounds every five minutes, and double this if the twin installation had been completed. The site was first detected in September 1943, with the construction of two railway tunnels about a mile apart.

Cheshire's Mustang, a Mosquito and seventeen Lancs headed in to the attack on the early afternoon of 6th July, and Cheshire marked the target from 800 feet in a dive attack. Although dropped on target they failed to show up at all well in daylight, but Munro led in the bombers as the sky became a nightmare of flak. Flying Officer Ian Ross's machine was hit and so was Stanford's. Flying Officer Lee had all four engines hit and three of his crew wounded from shell splinters and he had to jettison his bomb into the sea. Kell had an engine cut out on his first run but he turned for a second, dropping his bomb from 17,000 feet. Knilans made his run but the bombsight went u/s so he had to abort and head for home. Two other aircraft did not bomb as the crews could not identify the target.

The main hit, by Flying Officer Nick Ross, fell in the main area of the construction and caused a subsidence over an area of 160 by 120 yards. The roads and railways to the east of the tunnel entrance were completely severed. There was no chance of its being repaired and within a short while it was overrun by the advancing Allies. Later inspection of the site showed several Tallboy craters, one of which had pierced and blocked the tunnel in which labourers had been working. Several hundred of these workers were known to have been trapped in the tunnel, thinking it the safest place during an air raid.

This operation had been Cheshire's 100th trip. The AOC 5 Group, Ralph Cochrane, decided that was enough and he was taken off operational flying. He wasn't the only one to leave 617 at this time. Dave Shannon, Les Munro and Joe McCarthy, the three flight commanders, were all screened. These three had been with

617 from the beginning and this practically ended the link between those who had been the 'Dambusters' from those who had come afterwards.

Cheshire's place was taken by Wing Commander Willie Tait, and the flights were taken over by Squadron Leaders Fawke, T.C. Iveson and J.V. Cockshott. Willie Tait, from South Wales, ex-Cranwell was by now an experienced bomber pilot having flown with 51, 35, 10 and 78 Squadrons before joining 617. When he arrived he already held an impressive record of bomber ops. (one of the few with over 100 to his credit), as well as the DSO & bar and the DFC.

Low clouds over the Pas de Calais during July kept operations for 617 at a standstill, but on the 17th a fourth attack on Wizernes was mounted, with one Mustang, one Mosquito and sixteen Lancasters – Tait now flying in the Mustang. Over the target, Tait dived down to 500 feet to drop two red spot fires at 12.28 p.m., Fawke backing up with two more from 600 feet one minute later. As the Lancasters came in, Knights put his Tallboy on the north-west edge of the dome; Knilans' bomb fell fifty yards from the tunnel entrance, and Stout's landed just seventy yards away. Part of the cliff collapsed and then the roof fell in, blocking the tunnel. 617 returned to Wizernes on the 20th, although intelligence later showed it to have been unnecessary, but in the event bad weather caused the force to abort.

On the 25th they returned to Watten, although unknown to the British, the Germans had decided on the 18th to close it. Knilans made a direct hit, and others also scored well. A hit on the blockhouse caused the roof to fall off, trapping over 200 workers still there inside. Flight Lieutenant Fearn's bomber was hit by flak which severed his bomb release cable so they had to drop manually. Flying Officer Cheney's aircraft also received damage, wrecking his intercom. His mid-upper, unable to hear if they had real problems, decided to depart and baled out over enemy territory. The squadron received a congratulatory message from Bomber Harris when he saw the bombing photographs.

On the last day of July, 617 went to Rilly-la-Montagne which was a V-bomb storage depot set in a limestone cave near Rheims.

Two Mosquitos and sixteen Lancasters took off, backed up by Main Force units of Bomber Command. The one fear the crews of 617 had was that the bombing height of these other bombers were 18,000 feet, while 617 went in at 12,000 feet. Protests by 617 were disregarded and the plan stood.

Over the target several crews failed to bomb and Knilans had a scare. His engineer tapped him on the shoulder, saying, 'Look up above you, Skipper!' A hundred feet above was another 617 Lancaster, its bomb doors open. Knilans turned 'R' – Roger to one side using full rudder and a little aileron. His bomb aimer recovered quickly and soon found the A.P. again and sent their bomb to join several others in the target area. However, his starboard outer engine began overheating and he had to feather it which was the sixth time he had been forced to come home on three engines.

As they turned for home his rear gunner called, 'One of our aircraft has just had a bomb dropped on it.'

'Can you see any 'chutes?' asked Knilans.

'Not yet – oh, it's breaking up. There, I now see two 'chutes.'

The aircraft (ME557 'S)) was that flown by Bill Reid, VC. He had been flying in a loose gaggle formation, all the aircraft wanting to bomb quickly before the target was covered with smoke and before the Main Force aircraft came in. There was a good deal of flak and Mosquitos flying about taking photographs of the attack. Reid saw the target, made his run in, dropped his bomb and began to turn away when his bomb aimer said, 'Hold it, hold it.'

Bill Reid thought, 'There he goes again with his ruddy bombing pictures,' but levelled up as the camera took 28 seconds before it operated. After this length of time he suddenly heard 'boom, boom,' at the back of the aircraft. As feared, bombs had fallen from above and hit their Lancaster, one tearing through the fuselage, severing the control wires to the tail and elevators. After the first bump he ordered the crew to prepare to bale out, on the second bump he gave the order to go.

The engineer, 'Chunky' Stewart, handed Reid his parachute, but by this time the Lancaster had begun to spin out of control. Reid knew he must get out quickly, but getting out of his seat was easier said than done. The force of the spin was forcing the stick towards him but he finally made it and got to the dinghy escape hatch above him. As he turned to open it, the whole nose section seemed to be blown away because it suddenly disappeared and he found himself floating down through the air. He pulled his parachute open but kept a secure hold on the lines as he was not certain that he had securely locked the 'chute to his chest harness.

Below him he saw three trees coming up to meet him and kept his legs firmly together. He landed in one of the trees with a crack, his leg feeling numb as if it were broken. He slid down the tree, took off his Mae West and stuck it under a bush. His leg proved not to be broken but his hand appeared to be. His face was bleeding so he wrapped a shell dressing aircrew carried, to the wound. He could hear bombs exploding as the delayed action fuses went off so he knew he must still be near the target. His thoughts were to head south as he was only thirty miles from Paris and he knew enough French to get by. After a while he looked at his escape map but his plans were soon changed. A forceful challenge in German and three German soldiers, all carrying rifles with fixed bayonets, were standing looking at him.

He was ordered to raise his hands. A German came up to him and spoke in perfect English: 'You are one of the US forces.' He thought this because most daylight raids were carried out by the Americans and not the RAF. As he was marched away he saw the tailplane of his Lancaster and asked if he could take a look to see if anyone was alive in it. The turret was about 30 feet from the rear section and Hutton, the rear gunner, was still inside, his parachute streaming out. In the tail section he found Holt. He told the Germans their names so their next of kin could be informed.

Reid was taken to a small flak site where he sat on a bench to have his face and hand attended to by a doctor. About fifteen minutes later two guards came in with Dave Luker, his wireless operator, limping very badly. Luker remembered being thrown out of the aircraft and awoke on the ground with a German standing over him. They were the only survivors, all the others died including Les Rolton, DFC who had been with Reid when he won the VC. On their way to a POW camp, a German in Brussels noticed Reid's VC ribbon and said in German, 'Knight's Cross,' – the equivalent in Germany to the VC.

The Allied armies had now broken out of their beach-head positions and were nearing the sites that the RAF and 617 had been attacking. As each site was taken a report of the damage was sent back to Woodhall Spa. Watten had been so badly damaged that it had been abandoned, Wizernes had had its 10,000 ton dome knocked askew and its underground launching tunnels and living quarters caved in. (When the V2s began to rain on London in September they were fired from Holland.) Creil had all its limestone caves collapsed, the rockets stored there being buried under tons of earth. It had been the same at Rheims and at Siracourt the 16-foot concrete roof had been pierced. At Mimoyecques, the most dangerous site, with its two gigantic guns ready to fire V3 shells, had been smashed, its 20-foot roof now blocking the left-hand gun shaft.

At the end of August came the announcement that Leonard Cheshire had been awarded the Victoria Cross. He had flown four tours and 100 operations, many against Germany's toughest target. Although a raid on Munich was mentioned in his citation, his award was the first in this war not to be given for one specific act but for constant bravery over a prolonged period.

CHAPTER NINE

Return to the U-Boat Pens

Although 617's main targets were to be the U-Boat pens during August, the raid on the 1st was against Siracourt again; in the event cloud prevented bombing and the Lancasters brought their bombs home, having used 5,000 gallons of fuel for nothing.

On the 4th they went for the railway bridge at Etaples, about fifteen miles south of Boulogne, which crossed the River Canche. It was a vital link on the route for the German Army moving south-west from Courtrai, and a main route through to Belgium. Its destruction would delay supplies getting through to the Caen area where they were needed to prevent the Allies breaking out of Normandy after the British had pierced the central German line on 1st August.

No 617 Squadron was detailed to fly with 9 Squadron. It had not been the first, and certainly not the last occasion these two units would fly together, but this was the first against a specialised target. Fourteen Lancasters set off from 617, thirteen from 9 Squadron.

Willie Tait marked the target in the Mustang (HB937 'N') at 10.55 a.m. from 8,000 feet, with two 500 lb smoke bombs, and Duffy backed up in a Mosquito (NT205 'L'). Owing to a shortage of 12,000 lb bombs, the Lancasters carried 1,000-lb bombs. The supply of Tallboys had been reduced by the sustained effort against V-weapon sites and factories in England only produced around seven per week. Thirty were produced in America but they could be delayed by long sea crossings.

Flak at the bridge was light but accurate, but while the bombing appeared good, as the bridge was covered with smoke, photographs taken by Squadron Leader Rupert Oakley in a 627 Squadron

Mosquito showed the bridge to be hit but not broken.

The next day began the series of raids against the U-Boat pens. It was a daylight op, two Mossies and fifteen Lancasters with Tallboys heading for Brest. Tait marked with smoke bombs at 11.56 a.m. and the well-known heavy flak at Brest scoring hits on the Lancasters flown by Kell, Stout and Williams. There were at least five direct hits, three of which for certain penetrated the pens, and the breakwater to the west of the pens was smashed in two places.

As Knilans scored a direct hit his rear gunner, Roy Learmouth, called, 'Skipper, one of the Lancs behind is going down."

'Can you see the letter?' asked Knilans.

'I think it's V-Victor,' was his reply.

He was correct, it was V-Victor (JB139) piloted by 21-year-old Flying Officer Don Cheney, RCAF.

It was Don Cheney's 38th trip. He had dropped his bomb at exactly 12 noon having made a run straight and level at 18,000 feet for seventeen miles. During this run they flew through a terrific barrage, flak bursting all around the aircraft. Just after bombing there were three accurate bursts in quick succession, the last scoring an almost direct hit in the bomb bay. Both the navigator and wireless operator were severely wounded by fragments. The navigator, Pilot Officer Welch, on his 36th trip, was hit in the front teeth, upper lip and nose, as well as his arms and legs. Flight Sergeant Pool, on his 33rd op, was hit in the left temple, face, chest, both arms and both legs. Cheney asked for a new course, and although unable to speak, the wounded Welch showed the new course on his log sheet and passed it to Cheney. Then the engineer and bomb aimer gave the two men first aid.

As Cheney turned to port, the starboard outer engine failed and caught fire. It was feathered and appeared to go out. He then began to descend, since the oxygen masks of both wounded men were torn. Cheney then noticed a fire in the starboard wing and gave the order to bale out. The engineer put on the parachute for him as he came forward and tried to open the hatch, but the cover jammed. Helped by the navigator, they managed to manoeuvre it so as to leave just enough room to get through. Welch went out first followed by the engineer, Rosher, then Curtis, the bomb aimer. The mid-upper went out the rear exit.

As Curtis went past Cheney, he said, 'Reggie can't move.' Cheney pulled the Lancaster into a climb and attended to Pool in between going to and from the controls. In this way he succeeded in clipping on Pool's parachute and carrying him to the forward escape hatch. Cheney pushed him out, nodded, and Pool was able then to pull his own ripcord. Cheney dashed back to the cockpit, pulled the aircraft level for the last time but then the flames began breaking through the side of the fuselage burning his face and knee. It was now impossible for him to escape through the forward hatch, so he jettisoned the dinghy hatch and pushed himself through the top of the aircraft. He cleared the mid-upper turret and passed between the twin fins before pulling his 'D' ring.

The aircraft came down in a gentle spin emitting much flame and smoke to crash into the bay at Ste Anne-la-Palud. In 1972, on a visit to the area, Don Cheney was told by the local people that his aircraft could still be seen resting on the bottom in about 25 feet of water.

Welch, who had left the aircraft first, was shot by the Germans in his descent and was found on the shore by members of the French underground. Rosher landed by a roadside, was picked up by four Frenchmen before he had time to get out of his parachute, taken to a farm and given a drink before being hidden in a wood. Later he was taken in a car to join his colleague Porter, near Plonévez-Porzay, about thirty miles south of Brest. The rear gunner, Wait, who had also been wounded and had baled out was found dead in the sea off Douarnenez.

Pool's body was found by the French underground on the shore at Tréboul, being identified later by Cheney who had finally baled out at 5,000 feet. He landed in the sea, inflated his Mae West and discarded his parachute which sank at once. He was rescued about an hour later by a fishing boat manned by the Maquis while others held off the Germans with machine-gun fire. He was taken to Douarnenez and hidden in the home of A. Quebriac, then Commandant of the port. While there he was joined by Porter and Rosher. Welch, Pool and Wait were given a splendid funeral by the local people, attended by Cheney who remembered, 'It was one of the most moving things I have ever seen.'

Flight Sergeant Curtis landed in the sea in the bay and swam ashore. 'On reaching land I found five German soldiers waiting. They took me to Plogoff. I was later taken to a POW camp in Brest and was finally released by infantry of the 8th US Division on 18th September 1944.'

Cheney, Porter and Rosher were put in contact with the American 5th Armoured Division, east of Brest at the end of August, and then with British Intelligence at Bayeux where they were cleared and then flown back to England. Although Cheney had lost eight pounds in weight they were none the worse for their experiences. Cheney made a brief visit to 617 and then returned to Canada.

The return to attack on the U-Boat pens started in earnest on 6th August, the target on this date being Lorient. Two Mosquitos and twelve Lancasters found themselves over the target that evening, Tait marking from 8,000 feet right over the pens. To the Lancaster crews they looked like winking postage stamps, and then Fawke backed up with further marking despite heavy flak. This same flak damaged four Lancasters and another pilot had to jettison when he had an electrical fault.

Major overhauls were being undertaken at Lorient and a wet shelter made for U-Boat refitting. Four hits on the pens appeared to penetrate the roof, one near miss could be seen to the north-east corner, with another recorded between the dry and the wet pens. Once again the raid was photographed by 627 Squadron.

The squadron returned to Lorient the next day, just a small force of one Mosquito and nine Lancasters but the aircraft were recalled whilst over the target area, as it was believed that American troops were on the outskirts of the harbour. On the same day one of 617's Mosquitos crashed on the Wainfleet Sands Bombing Range; the pilot was Flying Officer Warren Duffy, DFC with Flying Officer Phil Ingleby as navigator.

Ingleby had volunteered to fly on a training flight with Duffy, who had flown over fifty bombing raids. They were practising target marking and it was to have been his last flight before going back to Canada. The Mosquito was the one in which Cheshire had marked Munich. As Duffy pulled up out of his attacking dive, a wing folded back and the aircraft crashed into the sea, both men being killed instantly. The notification of Duffy's DFC and his promotion to flight lieutenant came through on the day he died.

The target for the 9th was La Pallice. The weather was fine, making marking unnecessary and the bombing results were good and only Flying Officer Fearn was hit by flak, returning on three engines. They returned to La Pallice the next day, this time carrying six 2,000 lb bombs each. Flak was again heavy: four Lancasters were hit and Fearn again had to return on three engines. The results were judged good, many direct hits seen on the pens and the breakwater.

It was back to Brest on the 12th, Tait flying in a Lancaster of 617 for the first time on a raid. His aircraft, and three others all suffered under the heavy flak but again a number of direct hits made the raid a success. The main roof was pierced and a tanker, the *Rade*, was seen down by the stern at its moorings. Another tanker, the *Wat Kross* was seen on its side nearly submerged and half blocking the harbour.

The squadron made a return visit the next day. This time the target was an ex-French naval vessel, the *Gueydon*, which was being used as a blockship by the Germans. Despite being straddled by bombs, the ship was still afloat as the thirteen Lancasters flew off, but they had to return the next day.

This time they flew out in company with 9 Squadron who took 1,000-lb armour piercing bombs while 617 carried Tallboys. The journey out was uneventful. Although by this time the area surrounding Brest was occupied by Allied troops, Brest itself was still held by the Germans and the flak was as severe as ever, making life very uncomfortable for the bomber crews.

For the third time running Flying Officer Fearn was hit by flak and several other Lancasters damaged. Flight Lieutenant Pryor's aircraft (LM485 'N') was hit soon after his Canadian bomb aimer, Cecil Pesme, had dropped their bomb. A piece of shrapnel entered the nose compartment and hit Pesme in the throat as he was kneeling watching the bomb go down. The piece of shrapnel went through his throat and into his head, killing him instantly. When

Lloyd Pinder, the navigator, went forward to check on him he could feel the lump on top of his head where the shrapnel had lodged below his helmet.

Flying Officer Lee's machine (LM492 'W') was hit, Lee himself receiving a wound in the ankle, but he made a successful landing at Beaulieu. A recce flown on the 15th showed there was no sign of the blockship.

This proved to be the last trip for Flying Officer Dickie Willsher. On their return from Brest, 617 were stood down until 9 a.m. the next day, so Willsher and his crew went off to Boston for a drink, arriving back at Woodhall at midnight, only to find a note saying they were flying at 6 a.m. and that they would be called at 3 a.m. The next three hours was spent sobering up with coffee and cold water washes. Willsher and his crew then went on nine days' leave. When Willsher returned he broke out in cold sores in his mouth, styes on his eyes, carbuncles, and everything else one gets when one is run down. He left 617 on 2nd September after a spell in sick bay and was posted to No 5 LFS. He now lives in America.

On 16th August came a return to La Pallice in company with 9 Squadron. Three 617 aircraft took Tallboys, the rest of 617 and 9 Squadron carrying 2,000-lb bombs. Tait made his run and dropped his load of 2,000-pounders on what he thought was the target, seen through a small gap in the cloud. However, a few seconds later the AP was identified through another gap, and bombing was then abandoned because of the cloud. Flak was quite thick and Fearn had his Lancaster hit for the fourth time in succession.

As with so many other targets, failure on the 16th meant a return visit which took place on the 18th. Eleven Lancasters took off with one Mosquito and as before they carried a combination of Tallboys and 2,000-pounders. For the fifth time Fearn's Lancaster was hit by flak but despite extensive damage he managed to bring his aircraft back home. All bombs were released about the same time, although Knilans dropped his at 3.05 p.m., three or four minutes before the others. He was carrying an extra pilot on this trip, Flying Officer Joplin from New Zealand on his first operation with 617. Flying Officer Oram had an engine shot away over the target but still managed to bomb the pens and return home safely.

Photographs of the target later showed the bombing to be very successful.

On the 24th eight Lancasters bombed the U-Boat pens at Ijmuiden in Holland. They were escorted by Spitfires from 12 Group while a Mosquito gave photographic coverage. More success was achieved; more than one hit was seen on the entrance to the pens, three near the landside and two to seaward of the pens. One bomb penetrated the roof of the pens leaving a hole 15 feet in diameter, and two hits were seen on the rail tracks to the railway station in Fisher's harbour itself.

Three days later it was back to Brest yet again and again with 9 Squadron. 617 put up one Mosquito and twelve Lancasters whose specific target for their 1,000-lb bombs was a large merchant ship anchored alongside 'H' wharf which was thought to be intended for a blockship at some stage.

To attack it meant running the gauntlet of the whole harbour defences, but for some reason the guns were silent. This usually meant enemy fighters were about but none were seen. It was the easiest operation the squadron had had to date and more than one crewman noted in his log book – 'No flak!' The merchant ship was hit by 9 Squadron and seen to be blown at the stern after the raid, and another hulk blocking the harbour was also seen nearly submerged as they flew away.

Flight Lieutenant David Rodger, DFC, an original Dambuster, left the squadron during August, posted back to Canada – he had been McCarthy's rear gunner. Another to leave tour-expired was Flight Lieutenant Kearns, who had flown many marking ops in a Mosquito. He went to No 17 OTU.

Flight Lieutenant David Wilson left on a posting to 1661 Conversion Unit. Tragically he was killed in August 1947 while testing a prototype Avro Tudor II. On this test he was second pilot; soon after take-off the aircraft crashed, hit some trees and carried on into a lake. Also killed in the accident was Roy Chadwick, CBE, the designer of the Lancaster. The cause was later traced to an incorrect assembly of the aileron controls.

Joe McCarthy, another of the Dambusters, was another to leave 617 at this time, going to 61 Base. The squadron was changing – ever changing.

81

CHAPTER TEN

Tirpitz

The German battleship *Tirpitz* was launched at Wilhelmshaven on the 1st April 1939, the ceremony performed by the grand-daughter of Admiral von Tirpitz, Frau von Hassel, and in the presence of Adolf Hitler and his staff. It was February 1940, however, before trials were completed and *Tirpitz* began to become a menace and a threat. In fact though the Germans did not appreciate it, she became a menace and a threat without the need to sail from port. The disaster of convoy PQ17 in July 1942 was a prime example when the Admiralty gave the order to scatter the convoy since their intelligence could not positively confirm *Tirpitz* was still in harbour.

The ship was attacked on a number of occasions but in September 1943, came the start of a series of attacks at the end of which she finally met her doom. That same September 'Operation Source' was set in motion in which a force of midget submarines was sent out to attack the ship. The force was destroyed but the ship was damaged at her berth in Kaa Fjord, Norway. The following April the ship was attacked by the Fleet Air Arm and again damaged with 122 of her seamen killed and 316 wounded, yet the ship remained afloat and therefore a continued headache for the Admiralty.

The Navy and the FAA had attempted to sink it. Now it became the turn of the RAF. 5 Group were instructed to explore the possibilities of an attack and if possible to prepare a plan. There proved to be four main problems; weather, smoke screen, weapon and range. A close study was made of all the weather information available, and first hand evidence taken from Squadron Leader Furniss, DSO, DFC of 106 Group. He had flown many PRU sorties over the area of Norway where *Tirpitz* was now residing. All this information revealed that there was only about three days in the month of September 1944 when less than 3/10ths cloud was likely to be found.

The *Tirpitz*'s home in Kaa Fjord, an inlet fjord of the Alta, was narrow, steep-sided, and 1,000 miles from the nearest base in the British Isles. A Lancaster bomber with full petrol load could not fly to Kaa and back in one go even from the most northerly bases in Scotland. With a Tallboy bomb and full tanks, its all-up weight exceeded 67,000 pounds. Even with a Lancaster flying from Scotland with JW (Johnny Walker) bombs and full tanks, the weight exceeded 62,000 pounds. Thus it became essential to use an advanced base in Russia, and one near Archangel seemed most suitable.

The Germans had installed a highly efficient smokescreen system in Kaa Fjord. With this the FAA had found the whole area filled with a deep thick smoke. Surprise was essential as it took about ten minutes for the smoke to become an effective shield. By approaching from the south or south-east there was a chance of deceiving the efficient radar system existing in Norway around the Alten area. By approaching from this direction at high speed it was calculated the enemy would not get more than eight minutes' warning.

The weapon to be used was 617's Tallboys, the only bomb which could penetrate the ship's armour. The other weapon to be used was the JW bomb which had a weight of 4,000 lbs and 90 lbs of Torpex. It was designed on the principle of the oscillating mine for attacks on enemy shipping. The trim of the bomb was so adjusted that it moved vertically but sideways in water as well. If it hit the bottom of a ship on its upward path it would fire. On release from the aircraft the parachute opened by a static cord, and the safety pin was withdrawn from the fuse on impact with the water. The parachute released and fell away and in so doing pulled a flexible wire starting the gas to the fuse and cocked the self-destruction device. These would be dropped in a lake on the north side of the fjord which would be unaffected by the smoke screen around the ship.

At the end of August, Squadron Leader Eric McCabe of No 53 Base, Waddington, was approached by Air Commodore Hesketh with news that a special operation was being mounted. He told McCabe to assemble a small servicing party. Meanwhile, arrangements in Russia were under discussion. The runway at Vaenga, on the Volga, with a runway of 1,600 yards, was provisionally selected, but owing to the considerable fighter force at Murmansk and lack of accommodation and servicing facilities, it was decided to use Yagodnik airfield, some ten miles south of Archangel instead. The track mileage from Lossiemouth to Kaa and on to Yagonik was 2,100 miles, a distance which was considered feasible for a Lancaster with full tanks, and long-range tanks. These tanks, used in Wellington bombers, were fitted in the fuselage with one Mosquito type drop tank, which in total gave an addition 252 gallons. All the aircraft had their mid-upper turrets removed, and crewmen were to be carried at the discretion of the squadron commander.

Yet again 9 Squadron were to join forces for the attack and the total force was split into two groups, Group A of twenty-four aircraft (twelve each from both squadrons, and Group B of twelve (six from each squadron). There was also one film aircraft from 463 Squadron.

On 7th September, 511 Squadron at RAF Lyneham, whose normal role was mailing services to India and the Middle East, etc, were ordered to send two Liberator (C87's) aircraft to RAF Bardney, each with its five-man crew, for an indefinite period abroad. That their actual destination was Russia was not disclosed to the Captains, Flight Lieutenants Adams and Capsey, nor their crews. As most of the flights undertaken by 511 were to the tropics or at least to warm climates the men only took tropical kit with them!

Meanwhile, the Station Commander at Woodhall sent for the Station MO, Flight Lieutenant Matthews. To his complete surprise he was told he was going to Russia to look after some 200 men, for an indefinite period of between two and fourteen days. He would be responsible for health, food, recreation and First Aid.

All the aircraft were ready by the 8th but the plan had to be abandoned because it was evident that the short period of cloudless weather could not be forecast sufficiently ahead to enable the force to fly to Lossiemouth and then refuel to set off for the target. A decision, therefore, was made on the morning of the 11th to despatch the whole force direct to Yagodnik where it would refuel, refit and prepare to take off at the first opportunity to attack *Tirpitz*, all being dependent on the weather.

During the 9th and 10th, all sorts of rumours began about 617 Squadron. Nick Knilans received a new Lancaster, W-Willie, which had armour-plating under its engines, nitrogen self sealing tanks and a metered petrol gauge. He was asked to make short landing tests which he did by dragging the Lancaster in at low speed and low level. By doing this he was able to land in under 800 yards instead of the usual 1,200-1,600 yards. The exercise was to prove useful during the *Tirpitz* operation.

Squadron Leader McCabe, Chief Technical Officer at RAF Waddington, was busy selecting twenty-three groundcrew, representing several different trades. A large task lay ahead in packing up all the required equipment to keep thirty-seven Lancasters flying, and it included an engine change gantry, a 15-ton jack, exhaust stubs and a complete main wheel assembly.

Flight Lieutenants Adams and Capsey flew into Bardney on the 8th and were sent for by Air Commodore Hesketh. He told them the plan but they were not to tell their crews; however a message was sent back to Lyneham for warmer clothing.

Another briefing took place on this date; the floor of the briefing room at Woodhall was covered with a large-scale model of mountains encasing an inlet, but the attention was focused on a shelter under a sheer cliff, under which lay a model of the *Tirpitz*. It seemed a mammoth task with the distance involved, the smoke screening which might allow them only ten minutes in which to attack, and the expected flak from both ship and shore batteries.

On the night of the 10/11th, Wing Commander Wally Dunn, Chief Signals Officer at 5 Group, who had played an important part in 617's Dams Raid, was in his office at Group HQ with Air Commodore Sam Elworthy.[1] Here he had a special radio set – although special instructions were given to keep wireless silence. The Russians kept calling him but he was told not to answer. Fortunately the Germans appeared not to have heard them calling.

The final briefing was held on the 11th, when the weather appeared to be clear for the next week or so. Flight Lieutenant

[1] Now Marshal of the Royal Air Force Lord Elworthy.

Capsey remembers the navigation briefing having its funny moments. His navigator, Warrant Officer Spiller, DFM, was handed an enormous brief, from which, being a highly experienced navigator, he rejected the Gee charts, H2S, Oboe and other data, with the result that he was left, to the horror of the briefing officers, with only the colours of the day. It was at this briefing he heard the plan had been changed and that all the Lancasters were to fly to Archangel and operate from there.

Loading the aircraft presented a few difficulties, consisting of an extra Merlin engine, undercarriage leg and wheel, radio and radar spares and cases of tinned food which turned out to be a godsend. A corporal from 511 did a magnificent job in loading the Liberators with such a mixed bag, and then finding room for fourteen passengers. They were to fly from Lossiemouth.

Flight Lieutenant Matthews had a problem with water-sterilising tablets, having been able to scrape together only 100 tablets. He had made special arrangements for a further supply but they had not arrived.

Then over the Tannoy came the order for all Liberator crews and passengers to be in the aircraft by 6.30 p.m. and each passenger was issued with two blankets. The two Liberators arrived at Lossiemouth at around 8.25. In the meantime, the Lancasters of both bomber squadrons arrived as well as the photo Lancaster of 463 Squadron at Bardney.

One 9 Squadron aircraft, piloted by Flying Officer Lake, had a problem. Lake noticed a strange vibration and on investigation, the bomb aimer discovered that their bomb had slipped backwards, its tail back in the fuselage. They tried to dump it over the North Sea but it would not release, but then, by diving and pulling up sharply, it fell away, leaving Lake with little choice but to abort. 617 were all away from Woodhall, the first one being Bobby Knights (DV391 'O') at 6.51 p.m.

Having refuelled at Lossiemouth, the two Liberators took off at 9.30 while the Lancasters streamed out over the sea at a height of 400 feet to avoid the German radar, later climbing to around 8,000 feet to clear the mountains of enemy-occupied territory. Visibility was bad when later they had to fly over acres and acres of pine forests.

Flying Officer Carey and Flight Sergeant Sharp his mid-upper, remembered, 'We were flying at a height of about 14,000 feet. The flight was quite normal all the way over the North Sea, Norway and parts of Sweden until we flew over Finland when we came under heavy and light flak; evasion action was taken. I opened up from where the tracer was coming from (in the front turret), and the rear gunner, Gerry Witherick, also had a go at them. In the meantime we were hit several times.'

Another aircraft, this time of 9 Squadron, was also fired upon. Phil Tetlow in Flying Officer Macintosh's machine, recalls: 'We crossed Norway without mishap, but the Swedes decided to put on a little show for us. They fired shells off in all directions, some coming quite close.'

The visibility was appalling, and the crews only gained fleeting glances of the ground. Their immediate problem now was fuel. Most aircraft were getting dangerously low and the field at Yagodnik was proving a formidable task of location. At briefing, one navigator remembered the instruction – 'When you get to a large lake, with a railway viaduct crossing it, turn right.' Eventually most found the field but at times aircraft were down to 100 feet. It was not surprising that aircraft started to land with bits of foliage jammed in their tail wheel and elevator controls. Six aircraft crash-landed away from the main base, coming down at Varna, Vascova, Onega City and at Keg Island.

The problem of finding the field was put down to the weather forecast being inaccurate. It had been forecast that the lower cloud would be at 15,000 feet and visibility at Archangel would be six miles. This, combined with navigation problems caused by the confusion between the Russian and English alphabet, didn't help. The ground station callsign at Yagodnik was given as 8BP whereas it should have been 8WP. The Russian 'W' was the equivalent of the English 'B' as far as the alphabet was concerned but not as far as morse code was concerned. Also the only topographical map of the Archangel area didn't show enough detail to enable map-reading in such adverse weather conditions. Great credit was reflected on the navigators that they even reached Archangel, let alone Yagodnik.

The airfield was situated on an island on the River Dvina, some twenty miles south-east of Archangel. It was covered with grass but no properly laid out runways. Its normal role was as a Soviet Naval Air Force station whose prime job was to defend Archangel and shipping convoys in the White Sea.

The aircraft that came down elsewhere had run out of fuel, each pilot doing all he could to avoid crashing his aeroplane. When Flying Officer Ian Ross landed he had been searching for Yagodnik for some two hours. He finally selected a long stretch of wooden road for a landing. It was about 1,100 yards long. His first approach was too far to the right; the second was all right but a number of troops had stopped in the middle of it and were gazing up at them. The engineer reported only 30 gallons of petrol left so with this uppermost in his mind, Ross ordered the crew into crash positions, selected a marshy land stretch and approached at 115 mph. Keeping his tail well down he touched the ground without too many jars and the crew climbed out unharmed. However, in the landing the Tallboy bomb had detached itself and was lying 30-40 yards behind them. While Ross went to an American ship in the nearby harbour, Russian troops in the area put a guard on the bomb and aircraft.

Ross contacted Naval HQ and finally America House. A Lieutenant Morachell of the US Navy arrived and they left for British House where they were told to stay until Wing Commander Tait arrived.

Squadron Leader Wyness found a field with what appeared to be some fighter activity. He made a circuit and came in to land as close to the boundary as possible. The weather was poor and he could not see the opposite boundary of the field. After touching down he applied his brakes, but the ground was so wet it had no effect, with the result that the aircraft skidded along until it hit a fence, writing off the port undercarriage. However, everyone got out unhurt.

Flight Lieutenant Camsell and Flying Officers Morris, Keeley, Laws and Harris of 9 Squadron had similar incidents but all survived their forced landings without anyone being hurt. When Harris landed his aircraft it tipped up onto its nose so the Russians built a great haystack beneath its tail, then an army of men and women clambered along the fuselage, sat on the tail until their combined weight tipped the Lancaster back down onto the hay.

Then the Russians started to pull the haystack to pieces and slowly, as the stack got smaller, so the aeroplane's tail lowered itself back onto the ground.

Nick Knilans also had an eventful trip. He, like the others, found difficulty in locating the base but finally observed five boys of about ten years of age, signalling to him, which he gathered meant – land here. He and his crew had been flying for 12 hours and 30 minutes, the last ten minutes on 'empty' tanks. The field below was slightly downhill but Knilans, with the very last reserves of his fuel, dragged the Lancaster up the gulley, pulling up as he crossed a barbed wire fence. As his wheels crossed the fence he cut the throttles and plopped down onto a muddy field. Two engines cut out before they could be shut down and because of the mud and grass he could not keep the brakes on as this would have thrown the Lancaster sideways, breaking the undercarriage. The end of the field was coming up all too quickly but he eased the aircraft around a haystack and finally came to a halt near the boys.

Another Lancaster came in at a different angle, also out of petrol. This turned out to be that flown by Squadron Leader Tony Iveson. They all remained in their aircraft as it was drizzling outside, but all bombers leak to some degree and they began to get wet. Eventually a Russian jeep turned up and they climbed down to meet two Russian officers and a young woman in uniform. She, they found, was the interpreter, but she did not speak English! The Russians pointed out on a map that they had landed at Onega City.

They were taken across the muddy main street and into a log cabin. Being all very thirsty by this time they kept asking for water, when in came a white-coated waiter carrying a tray full of water tumblers. Paddy Blanche was so parched he drank his down in one gulp. Then he went white, and yelled:

'It's bloody Vodka!'

They were then served a meal of meaty soup, black bread and tea. The camp they were in turned out to be a rest camp for survivors from Stalingrad.

Wing Commander Tait arrived in style in an ancient Russian biplane, which he later described as looking like a coffin. During the day a Russian Douglas DC3 cargo plane, with the American white star painted out, arrived with a small quantity of 100-octane gasolene but just enough to get the two Lancasters to Yagodnik. The Russians had turned the aircraft around by hand but with the brakes still full on! Little wonder it took a lot of men, as the interpreter told Don Bell.

Tony Iveson took off first and made for the White Sea, having a lighter bomb load. Knilans then bumped across the field with the Merlins on full emergency power and lifted off at the water's edge, then turned for Yagodnik. Knilans called for 'Wheels up', but the engineer, wanting to be helpful, pulled up the flaps instead, causing the Lancaster to sink several feet. It was enough to drop the aircraft into the tops of the pine trees and for some while they ploughed their way through the treetops. Knilans could not pull up too quickly as this would drop the tail assembly further into the trees. A small valley was ahead and he thought that if he kept going he could fly out of the treetrops and then climb. Paddy Blanche, in the rear turret, reported treetops snapping up straight behind him.

Then a lone pine tree loomed ahead, towering several feet above the others. Knilans knew it would damage the propellers if he hit it, so made a flat skid sideways to make the nose of the aircraft take the impact. It crashed into the tree, smashed the perspex, destroyed the bomb sight, shattered the cockpit windscreen, then ripped off the bomb-doors. Don Bell's maps etc, were blown out via the rear turret and later a piece of tree, three feet in length, was found by the main door. This later resided in the Mess at Woodhall with the caption 'Believe it or not'. It now resides in Australia in the home of Roy Learmouth, one of the crew. He also made a model Lancaster from the broken perspex collected from inside the nose.

Meanwhile, the starboard engine radiator quickly filled with pine needles and overheated, forcing Knilans to shut it down. They were flying at 150 mph with a violent stream of air rushing into the shattered nose. The hatch over the pilot's head was forced open and the wind rushed in through the nose, past the pilot and out of the escape hatch. It took everything that was not screwed down, such as maps, the wireless operator's cap, etc; Knilans was having to fly with one hand while his other hand was over his eyes, but he managed to peer through slightly separated fingers.

The rest of the 60-mile journey was comparatively uneventful.

They landed at Yagodnik on three engines with extreme difficulty as some of the controls were jammed and the main frame appeared to have been twisted. On arrival the briefing for the attack on the *Tirpitz* was on and they rushed in, Don Bell with his hair full of pine needles and debris. The haste was in vain. The target area was clouded over and the attack was postponed until the next day.

Squadron Leader Cockshott had landed at Vascova and become bogged down. Squadron Leader McCabe flew over in what appears to have been the same biplane or a similar one as used by Tait. It had three instruments in the front cockpit, a wooden seat, a top speed of 60 knots and navigation was by following the railway lines. He arranged for 100 men, with the help of a Major Kirjanov, to pull the Lancaster out of the mud. They appeared to find it very difficult but this was not surprising – all the time they had been pulling it up the runway, they too had left the brakes on.

The PRU Mosquito of 540 Squadron, took off from RAF Benson on the 12th, piloted by Flight Lieutenant George Watson and navigator Warrant Officer John McGregor MacArthur. They landed at Yagodnik only to find there had been no mention of a Mosquito to the ground crew, so they had no spares available for it. The Russians clearly admired the aeroplane very much. Flying Officer Tweddle of 9 Squadron remembers it as being light blue and a beautiful sight sitting on the airfield at Yagodnik. Its role was to provide visual and photographic recce information of the *Tirpitz*, and report on the weather.

Both Liberators arrived in Russia, one landing at Keg Island, the other, together with the PRU Lancaster of 463 Squadron, flown by Flight Lieutenant Bruce Buckham, landing at Yagodnik. Later the first Liberator flew over to Yagodnik.

The senior RAF officer on the operation was Barney's Station Commander, Group Captain C.C. McMullen, AFC. When he arrived at Yagodnik he was met by the Russian Base Commander. Stretched out on the walls of a hut prepared for the RAF was a banner which read: 'Welcome the glorious fliers of the Royal Air Force.' The Russians had expected some 250 RAF personnel but in fact the number was 325. The accommodation was, in the circumstances, comfortable, the officers had the paddle-steamer *Ivan Kalyev* on the river, which was the only access to the field from

Archangel. The remainder of the men and a surplus of officers were put in an underground set of quarters about a quarter of a mile from where the HQ hut had been set up. The biggest problem was bed-bugs! Messing was reasonable and Flying Officer 'Mac' Hamilton recalls that at breakfast pilot officers and flying officers got one egg, a flight lieutenant two, squadron leaders three and a wing commander got four. What Group Captain McMullen received is anyone's guess!

While waiting for good weather for an attack, the Russians laid on some entertainment, including a football match; their side came fully kitted out whereas the RAF team had to play in what they wore. It seemed a pretty professional team from Moscow who seemed to use substitutes at will. Although the Russians won, the score appears to vary according to whom one asks. A visit to Archangel was also arranged and many of the crews sampled the local Vodka a little too well and became rather the worse for wear. On the way home a Canadian wireless operator decided to take a dip in the river, but he was soon picked up by a Russian launch, taken back and put to bed.

The ground crews were performing miracles of repair and maintenance work under difficult conditions. Using some spare parts from Lancasters too badly damaged in the arrival crashes, other aircraft were made serviceable including Knilans' machine. Refuelling was another problem. Bowsers with a capacity of 4,000 gallons had been promised but those available only held between 300 and 400 gallons, so it took over 18 hours to refuel the total force. Meanwhile, the PRU Mosquito flew a recce on the 14th and again on the 15th. Its return from the latter brought a favourable report – the raid was on!

The force was now down to twenty-seven Lancasters, twenty-one with Tallboys, six with Johnny Walker mines, and as they took off the Russians all turned out to see them off, a band playing the 'Conquering Hero'. They flew low in a gaggle, like seagulls after a fish, and at less than 1,000 feet to avoid German radar. One Lancaster flew 1,000 feet above the rest, but radio silence kept Tait from calling him down to the level of the rest.

They had a scare over Finland when they flew over a large

German air base. The runway lights were on but no aircraft could be seen on the ground or in the air. They thought there must be one or two squadrons in the area and without a mid-upper turret and with front and rear turrets only, they were a little apprehensive.

Ten minutes from the target the pilots put on emergency boost power with their Mark 24 engines. The best bombing height on this op for the Tallboy was 11,500 feet. Reaching the locality of the *Tirpitz*, the enemy had been alerted and had started the smoke pots on the hills around the ship. About eight minutes from target the flak started up. Many of these were situated on the hills and high ground, the Lancasters running through a black curtain of exploding AA shells. Then the ship's guns opened up, which in fact improved the aiming point for the bomb aimers.

Three of the 9 Squadron aircraft were acting as windfinders and were flying slightly above the rest of the force until they got to about sixty miles from the ship when they dropped behind, as the others put on emergency power for the run in. The plan was to produce a pattern of bombing of approximately 750 yards. The Johnny Walker aircraft had three aiming points, two to the north and one to the south.

The local German fighter station was at Bardufoss where JG5 had its base. The CO was Major Heinrich Ehrler, a heavily decorated fighter pilot from the Russian front, where he had scored 204 kills and held the Knight's Cross with Swords and Oakleaves. However, it had not been felt necessary for fighter cover at Kaa Fjord as the smoke screen was thought to be good enough protection.

The plan of attack was to approach in four waves of five aircraft in line abreast, each occupying 1,000 feet in height with a distance between waves of a few hundred yards. The direction of the attack was from the south along a fore and aft axis of the *Tirpitz*. The JW aircraft bombed from a height of 10-12,000 feet in two waves and attacked across the target from south-east to north-west.

Flak scored hits on several of the Lancasters as they came in. Knilans lost an engine after dropping his bomb; his starboard outer began to overheat as he did so; but he waited until after the attack before shutting it down. He returned to Yagodnik and made his seventh three-engine landing. Flying Officer Oram was hit by flak which damaged the tailplane, making rudder and elevator controls useless. Because of this he could not turn the aircraft and was heading steadily for the North Pole! However, as the flak died away, vibration set in and they were gradually able to turn for Yagodnik.

Out of the seventeen Tallboys dropped, 617 dropped eleven. Squadron Leader Cockshot and Flight Lieutenant Knights failed to locate the ship in the smoke and so brought their bombs back. Flight Lieutenant Mac Hamilton had a hang-up and the bomb eventually dropped away four miles south of the ship. 617 also let go forty-eight JW mines. Two other aircraft returned damaged.

Both squadrons used completely different types of bomb sights. 9 Squadron used the Mark 14, which was controlled by a computer box into which one automatically fed the compass course and air speed. If the wind velocity and direction fed into the box was absolutely correct the bomb sight would also be correct, so it was vital that a dead accurate wind was found, hence the windfinder force. 617 used their SABS. The sight could be corrected during the bombing run and provided it was correct on release, the bomb would not over or under shoot the target.

The whole attack was filmed by the PRU Lancaster (LM587 'L'), and this film is today kept in the Imperial War Museum in London. On board was Guy Byam, a BBC War Correspondent, later to be lost over Berlin on a daylight raid with the 8th US Air Force on 3rd February 1945. Byam was always talking about his next mission, which on this occasion turned out to be Arnhem. Another passenger in the Lancaster was W.E. West also a war correspondent of the Associated Press. The cameraman, Flying Officer Eric Giersch, an Australian, was operating from the mid-upper turret. There were two other cameramen from a film unit, Flying Officer Loftus and Pilot Officer Kimberly. After the attack they flew straight back to Waddington, arriving at 10 p.m., a trip of over 14½ hours.

A Mosquito took off at 2.10 p.m. and returned four hours later, attempting to take photographs but low cloud covered the whole fjord. However, the pilot was able to see the ship from 9,000 feet through a gap in the clouds. German Intelligence reported the sinking of three minor vessels but no damage to the *Tirpitz*. On the 19th they changed their minds, and then admitted that the ship had been hit forward by a heavy bomb. On the 25th, Admiral Dönitz reported: 'After successfully defending herself against many heavy air attacks, Battleship *Tirpitz* has now sustained bomb hits, but by holding out, her presence confounds the enemy's intelligence.'

In fact, a bomb had gone through the upper deck to emerge well below the waterline on the starboard side before exploding. Damage reported was the flooding of the forward part sections. In order to be seaworthy again there would be an estimated nine months of repair work.

The first hit claimed on the ship was by 9 Squadron, Flying Officer Melrose in aircraft 'J', at 10.55 a.m. The next was a 617 aircraft, Flight Lieutenant Pryor, one minute later, then Squadron Leader Fawke at 11.09. A hit by Wing Commander Tait was not plotted but it was thought to have been a hit or a very near miss. Near misses were also recorded by Knilans and Flying Officers Kell, Oram and Stout. The Russians were disappointed that the ship had not been sunk, but in the circumstances both squadrons had done well.

On the 16th the Mosquito once again took off to film the *Tirpitz*, but yet again they found cloud over the area. When it descended to get a better view, the flak became too intense to stay around. The Mosquito returned with five flak holes and repairs had to be made on the staboard drop tank, fuselage and starboard engine. Also on the 17th, sixteen aircraft took off to return to the UK. Tait led Iveson, Fawke, Castognola, Sanders, Stout, Pryor, Gingles, Levy and Cockshot; the other aircraft were from 9 Squadron. Sadly, Flying Officer Frank Levy (PB416 'V') crashed in the mountains at Rukkedalen (Saurest) in Norway. They hit a steep hill not far from the top; pieces of wreckage were spread over a large area and some of these can still be seen in a small museum near where the Lancaster crashed. From eye-witness accounts, the bomber appeared to develop engine trouble, and the aircraft dropped flares before it crashed.

The Norwegians put up a wooden cross at the crash site and the bodies of the crew were buried in a mass grave by the Germans. Levy, a Rhodesian, was taking back two of Wyness's crew, Flying Officer James Naylor and Flying Officer Denis Shea, DFC. These two men were buried with their comrades in arms.

The following day Watts, Kell, Howard, Hamilton, Knilans left for England, with Oram and Carey on the 18th with three of 9 Squadron. Perhaps in a moment of gay abandon, someone in one of these five Lancasters fired off two Very flares from 50 feet on take-off. Unfortunately they set some of the woodland on fire, which amused the Russians not at all.

The final two aircraft took off on the 20th, Cockshott and one 9 Squadron machine. The ground crews had to stay on for a while, finally returning a week later. Some names of 617's ground personnel are worthy of mention for without them the operation would have been impossible: Sergeant L. Cooper, Sergeant J. Sherman, Sergeant C.L. Little, Sergeant R.A. Boreland, Sergeant J.F. Peters, Flight Sergeant J. Cherankora and Corporals F.W. Tyzack, J.P. Overton and Kelly; also the ground crews of 9 Squadron under Flight Sergeant Hopgood and the Russian staff under Major Kirjanov.

The *Tirpitz* raid was the last trip of Lieutenant Nicky Knilans. He had flown twenty trips with 619 and now a further thirty with 617 Squadron, all from RAF Woodhall Spa, and spanning the period May 1943 to October 1944. He had been awarded a DSO and DFC by the British and the American DFC and Air Medal by his own country. On return to Woodhall, via Lossiemouth, his Lancaster was towed away for scrap. He remembers stripping off all his clothes on return to the courtyard of the Petwood Hotel and burning them before going in for a bath and clean clothes.

There were obviously few awards for the attack, but DFCs did go to the Mosquito crew who had flown eight recce sorties over *Tirpitz* during the period in Russia. They were Warrant Officer John McArthur and Flight Lieutenant George Watson, who in total had flown some thirty-five missions while with their squadron. A DFC also went to Flight Lieutenant Melrose of 9 Squadron who was credited with hitting the battleship with his bomb. On 30th September, Air Commodore Hesketh received a signal from

Admiral Sir Henry Moore, C-in-C Home Fleet:

I would like to convey to the crews concerned my appreciation of the great effort ... [I] can appreciate the difficulties and hazards involved. I will be glad if you would pass this to the crews who took part in this operation which from the photographs taken show that damage has been inflicted on the last major unit of the German Fleet.

CHAPTER ELEVEN

Operations Continue

There was no respite for the squadron upon their return to England from Russia. Their first assignment was to return to the Dortmund-Ems Canal on 23rd September, still one of the most important waterways in Germany, linking the Ruhr with the North Sea. In September 1944 it was a vital link for German forces that had encircled Arnhem where the British Airborne forces were having a bitter fight.

The squadron was accompanied by 125 Lancasters of 5 Group, carrying 1,000-lb bombs while 617 took Tallboys. Five Mosquitos of 627 Squadron were detailed to do the target marking. The object of the operation was to breach the banks of the canal, at a point where the level of the water was above the surrounding countryside. If breached it would drain the canal. To do this, 617 needed to drop their Tallboys from at least, and preferably above, 8,000 feet.

The Mosquito aircraft were led by Squadron Leader Rupert Oakley. He flew in DZ633 and dodged the flak, flying the length of the nearby defences to drop his incendiary markers. He remembers it as 'being a little hot at the time!' For this attack he received an immediate DFC to add to his DFM won with 61 Squadron in 1940. He was later awarded the DSO and the AFC in 1956.

Conditions over the target were difficult because cloud covered the canal at 8-9,000 feet. The first 617 aircraft in was Tony Iveson. He saw the markers clearly and dropped his bomb at 9.45 p.m. He was followed by Flying Officer Phil Martin who saw the TIs from 8,000 feet. Squadron Leader Wyness followed, made three good runs but each time cloud obscured the target; he went down to 12,000 feet, made another unsuccessful run and brought his bomb home. Flying Officer Sanders did likewise, but Cockshott bombed;

so too did Willie Tait, from 7,500 feet and Flight Lieutenant Hamilton from 8,000. Flight Lieutenant Sayers made five runs but by this time the markers had burnt out and with a u/s compass his efforts went unrewarded, but Castagnola and Oram did bomb successfully.

Flight Lieutenant Geoff Stout was jumped by night fighters shortly after leaving the target. He lost three engines, both of the port ones and the starboard inner. Flight Sergeant Peter Whittaker in his mid-upper turret heard cannon shells hitting the aircraft; then the pilot put the bomber into a corkscrew manoeuvre – the standard evasive tactic when being attacked by a night fighter. Climbing from his turret, Whittaker saw flames coming from the bomb bay and then saw that they now had only one engine. Having failed to bomb, they still had their Tallboy aboard but when they tried to jettison it the release lever came away in the bomb aimer's hand. Whittaker then opened the bomb bay hatch and saw flames all around the bomb. Flying Officer Graham, the navigator, had been badly wounded and he was pulled to one side and a parachute fixed to his harness. They pulled his rip-cord and pushed him out of the aeroplane.

Whittaker went forward and discovered that Stout had no parachute – it had probably been used for Graham – so he went aft, found him a spare and clipped it to his pilot. Stout then ordered Whittaker out, indicating that he would follow, but he was never seen alive again. On the way down, Whittaker heard the Lancaster and could see fire underneath it. At the same time he heard a twin-engined aircraft circling, which was probably the Me110 that had hit them.

Whittaker landed safely but was unable to bend his arm; he discovered that he had been wounded in the elbow, and he was also bleeding from a head wound. He decided to make for the area south-west of Arnhem. Flying Officer Bill Rupert, aged twenty from Toronto, was on his 32nd trip; when he landed, he broke a bone in his right foot and right shoulder. He eventually found a Dutch farmhouse and met up with Whittaker.

Pilot Officer Allan Benting, the engineer, died in hospital in Enschede on the 25th and was buried there. The wounded navigator, the son of Major-General Sir Miles Graham, did not make it and was buried at Oostobeak Cemetery, Holland. Geoff Stout died when his aircraft crashed and was buried in Lochem Cemetery. Flying Officer Ronald Allen, the wireless operator, baled out and was taken prisoner.

The other gunner, Flying Officer Reg Petch, also baled out successfully and evaded capture. He had previously been with 76 Squadron when commanded by Leonard Cheshire, had been Gunnery Leader and even flown with Cheshire. He made it back to England, and so too did Rupert and Whittaker; in the case of Rupert, however, it wasn't until 1945 as he stayed with the Resistance forces helping in sabotage work. He eventually arrived back on 617 on the eve of the squadron's last operation of the war and immediately asked to go on it. He was given permission, but the then CO said he had done enough and permission was refused.

Tony Iveson flew alongside Stout's Lancaster earlier that day, himself in a Mustang. They had been flying a practice fighter affiliation and Tony later felt that Stout had had something on his mind – perhaps a premonition of what was to come.

As a result of the attack, over ten miles of the canal was drained, cutting off the Ruhr waterways from the North Sea and Berlin. Over twenty-three barges were left stranded and over 4,000 workers needed to be employed in rebuilding both banks for a distance of some two miles. A safety gate, which should have been capable of shutting off the water in emergencies, was rendered completely unserviceable by a near miss. Thus for six months, Bomber Command and 617 denied the enemy its most important gateway for transporting stores, coal, iron ore etc, to and from the Ruhr.

Ten aircraft were detailed for an op. on 3rd October when a force of 247 Lancasters with 4,000 and 1,000 lb bombs attacked Westkapelle, the greater part of which was below sea level. The target was the sea wall, but in the event 617's Tallboys were not required and thus recalled.

The next target brought memories of the past. It was the Kembs Dam, 6½ miles north-west of Basel which governed the flow of the Rhine between the Swiss town and Strasbourg. If the Allies did not destroy it the Germans would, but the Americans wanted it destroyed in good time for the waters of the Rhine as far north as Strasbourg, to subside by the time they were ready to cross it. Requests from the 9th US Air Force to the 5th HQ Bomber Command, resulted in orders to 5 Group to destroy the dam at the earliest moment. The date was set for 6th October but owing to the weather, this was postponed to the 7th.

The Germans held the view that a continuous flood wave would be caused by the rapid opening of the Kembs Weir sluices and would last several hours, although it would gradually subside as it passed downstream. It would affect the water levels as far as Mascau, approximately opposite Karlsruhe. The power station would be seriously endangered and its working paralysed. This opening was to be carried out in agreement with the Swiss authorities if infringement of Swiss territorial rights were to be avoided. The gates were operated electronically on a principle similar to that of a sashed window. The danger to attacking infantry was obvious if the Germans had power to open the sluices in the event of an American attack.

On the 7th, thirteen aircraft of 617 took-off carrying Tallboy bombs, seven of which had 25-second fuses. These seven were to be dropped from high level and the other six, with 30-minute fuses, from low level, 500-800 feet. The force was escorted by three Mustang squadrons, 315 Polish Squadron, led by Wing Commander Jan Zumbach, DFC, 129 Squadron and 306 Polish squadron. As in the past a photographic Mosquito went along from 627 Squadron. The force made rendezvous at Dungeness and when they reached the target the weather was clear with good visibility but the defences proved to be far more formidable than had been expected. An intense light flak was experienced, mainly coming from the eastern bank of the river. The run up to the dam was a long one, to be precise, four miles. The defence at the dam itself was light, but at the power station, which was sighted on the run up, the defence was formidable.

One bomb fell immediately beyond the barrier and there were two overshoots of 40 to 50 yards by Flying Officers Watts and Martin. Another bomb fell close to the westernmost sluice gate and demolished it. This was very likely the one dropped by Castagnola. Willie Tait's bomb was seen to explode and blow open the sluice gates, releasing the pent-up water.

On his run into the target, Flight Lieutenant Christopher 'Kit' Howard, called over the radio, 'I'm going through now.'

Flying Officer Phil Martin replied, 'Hold it, Kit, I'll go through with you.'

Whether he heard Martin's call or not or just decided to make his run is not known, but half way to the target, surrounded by flak, fire was seen belching from a damaged port engine. Moments later the left wing of his Lancaster ripped away and the aeroplane fell away, crashed into a wood and exploded. They were all killed. Howard was of the Howard family, whose home was Castle Howard, Yorkshire – he was twenty-two.

The explosion from Howard's aircraft upset Martin's bombing run and the bomb aimer told Martin to go round again. Martin pulled up the Lancaster in the direction of the Swiss border through the smoke and flames. His rear gunner, Trebelcock, was blazing away at the ground defences as they went. On the second run, Don Day, the bomb aimer, let go their bomb which he claimed as a hit, but in fact overshot. The aircraft was then hit at the rear end and Martin said he had poor control. Blagborough, the engineer, went to the rear of the Lancaster and found the rudder wire broken. He picked up the fire axe which was kept in the rear fuselage, plugged himself into the intercom wrapped the axe round the wire and gave the pilot what assistance he could when it was required.

One of Tait's gunners commented, 'We are copping all kinds of hell from flak.'

Tait replied, 'I guess we are over the power station.'

Squadron Leader Drew 'Duke' Wyness's machine was seen to be hit repeatedly as he made his bomb run and have an engine on fire. Despite this he managed to complete the run, drop his bomb before falling away to crash in the Rhine, near Bellingen, Germany. He and his crew were able to inflate the aircraft's dinghy and they began to paddle towards the Swiss side of the water. However, the Germans on the opposite side opened up with machine-guns, killing all the occupants of the dinghy, which was witnessed by a Swiss lock keeper and also by a man fishing in the canal.

Flying Officer Sayers, an Australian, saw Wyness shot down as he was making a second run. As he opened his bomb doors as the target came up, an electrical fault caused his bomb to release prematurely.

It was hard for the other crews to take in that only a few hours before Wyness and Howard, with their crews, had all been very much alive and with them at Woodall. Bob Barry, of Sayers' crew, remembers seeing Wyness going into the face of the most frightening barrage of light and medium flak they had ever seen during the war.

The last crew to bomb was that of Flying Officer Freddie Watts, who took off after the rest, but finally caught up with the squadron over the target. Over the Swiss border they had their starboard outer engine blown out by Swiss gunners. Front gunner, Gerry Witherick, was covered with bits of perspex and oil, but his pilot carried on and bombed, their Tallboy overshooting by 50 yards. Watts' determination on this raid was mentioned in his citation for a subsequent DFC in December 1944, together with that of his bomb aimer, Pilot Officer McKay when he received his DFC.

Flight Lieutenant Tice, in the 627 Squadron Mosquito, took photographs of the damage to the gates and later reported:

The water above the dam was placid and undisturbed. Below the barrier there was little water in the river bed and I could see the sandy bottom clearly. We circled above the clouds and were about to turn for another run when there was a terrific explosion. The water went up in a column about 1,000 feet high. We circled again and were about to leave when there was a second explosion. I saw the dam cracking and water started to pass through a breach in the western end.

The quiet water above the barrier broke into a ripple which became a torrent as more and more water poured through the breach. The strike photos showed direct hits as well as near misses. The two bombs that Tice saw explode had been two set with 30-minute fuses. The water level receded and 2½ miles upstream it fell eleven feet and many barges were left stranded. The iron superstructure above the first and second pillars on the west side had been completely destroyed together with the sluice gates.

Flying Officer Phillip Martin was awarded an immediate DFC for this operation and four other awards mentioned the Kembs dam operation. Flying Officer Walter Daniel, Tait's bomb aimer, who had flown on thirty-four raids, and whose bomb was seen to explode on the sluice gates, received the DFC, and Flying Officer Sanders received a bar to his DFC. Squadron Leader John Cockshott later received a bar to his DFC, and Warrant Officer Dennis 'Mickey' Vaughen also collected a DFC.

The fighter escort also suffered losses totalling seven aircraft, all, it is believed, from ground fire. Three of those lost came from 306 Squadron; 315 and 129 each lost two, but they probably all landed safely in France.

Towards the end of October, the battleship *Tirpitz* was back on 617's target list. From a former member of the *Tirpitz*' crew, now a prisoner, it was learned that the attack of 15th September had had considerable success. A near miss by a Tallboy close to the forecastle, grazed the side of the vessel, pushing in the ship's wall, with the result that the water level rose to the torpedo bulkhead. This bomb had sealed the ship's fate.

Tirpitz was patched up provisionally and, on 16th October, towed to Tromso Fjord at a speed of less than 7 knots. The move could possibly have been because the Germans feared the ship falling into the hands of the Russians who were rapidly over-running the Petsamo area, or possibly they wished by stages to get her back to a German base, where major repairs and a re-fit could be carried out.

She was berthed between Haskoe Guidoy on the 18th, then towed through Sandisund to Haakoy. The island of Haakoy was four miles west of Tromso and the move had brought her some 200 miles nearer to Britain. By coincidence on the 18th, an armed reconnaissance was flown by seven Firefly aircraft of No 1771 Squadron of the Fleet Air Arm of HMS *Implacable*; their task was to seek out enemy shipping in the Tromso area. They reported back that the *Tirpitz* was there, together with an anti-aircraft ship, three destroyers and a repair vessel. Confirmation was quick in coming when a Mosquito of 540 Squadron flew a search mission for the battleship and found her the same day.

Unknown to the Allies was that the hole in the ship's side had been filled with sifted spail, and the ship became, owing to her having been anchored in 50 feet of water rather than left to rest in shallow water, a floating gun battery to help protect German position in Norway. As the ship appeared to still be active, and therefore a continued threat, another plan was devised to attack her by 9 and 617 Squadrons.

The round trip to the ship's new position was 2,252 miles. It could just be done, but to achieve it all the Lancasters had an engine change. The ground crews changed some 120 engines (Merlin 24s) within a few days, which gave each a boost of plus 18 for take-off with the all-up weight. One Wellington long-range fuel tank was slid inside the fuselage by temporarily removing the rear turret, and a Mosquito drop tank was added. This gave a total fuel load of 2,406 gallons. To reduce the overall weight, the mid-upper turret was again removed, also the armour plating around the pilot, and the ammunition supply was greatly reduced. The force would refuel in Scotland – the overall code word was 'Operation Obviate'.

Nineteen Lancasters drawn from both squadrons took off from Lossiemouth on the 29th October, refuelled and were away by 1 a.m., heading towards Norway. They crossed the hostile coast where radio location detectors were known to be inefficient, then headed on towards Sweden to make rendezvous above a lake before they turned on a final leg that took them to Tromso. Over the lake, five aircraft of 9 Squadron, acting as wind finders set off in loose formation, climbing steadily. Ten miles from Tromso they left the formation to find the wind, then radioed their findings to the leader, but something appeared to be going wrong as the leader of 617 was telling them to go round again. The problem was patches of cloud that were drifting over the ship, hiding it completely, except for brief glimpses of the ship's guns blazing up at them.

As on the first trip via Russia, a PRU Lancaster of 463 Squadron was in attendance, and the pilot was again Bruce Buckham. He descended from 14,000 to 8,000 feet and saw the first bombs burst about 100 yards from the ship. Two more bombs struck the nets surrounding the target. In some cases the pilots made several bomb runs from different directions, but the weather conditions gradually deteriorated. The final view of *Tirpitz* showed her to be still afloat and with all her guns firing.

The gunfire had hit Flying Officer Carey's machine, knocking out its starboard outer and causing a petrol leak. Descending to get away, he crossed the little fishing village of Andenes, where another burst of gunfire hit a petrol tank and stopped the left inner engine. With two engines out and with a severe loss of fuel, they were not going to make Scotland. To make matters worse, their hydraulic system had also been hit causing their wheels, flaps and bomb doors to drop. The resultant drag made the aircraft barely flyable and to try to maintain any sort of height, the two remaining engines were being run at maximum revs.

The crew considered ditching but the sea looked too rough. All the time they had been putting out a 'May Day' call with the hope of contacting the Navy destroyers which were supposed to be standing by along their return route. They heard no reply and Gerry Witherick, whose brother was in the Navy, commented: 'Where the hell is the bleedin' Navy when you need them? I shall have to talk to my brother about this!'

Carey said, 'We can't ditch and we can't get home, so it's over the mountains to Sweden.'

Gerry replied, 'This can't happen to me, it will ruin my reputation. I always get home.'

Carey said, 'Can't it? You watch.'

They set course for Sweden, throwing out loose equipment such as guns, ammo, etc, to lighten the aeroplane, also anything that could be classified material went out through the open bomb bay. Soon the cloud-swept peaks of the Norwegian mountains loomed ahead. After a while Carey managed to find a passage through the range and somehow guided 'E-Easy' through them. For miles they struggled along over steep peaks and deep lakes. Then they were over Sweden, with no fear of German POW camps, but it was only a matter of time before both engines seized up.

Near Porjus, a small Lapland village, they spotted a field which looked frozen hard and decided to try and land with wheels up. They cranked them up by hand, then with the crew in their crash positions Carey brought them in. As it hit the ground, the bomber skidded along the ground; then it suddenly stood up on its nose, then with a crash fell heavily back again. It was ten hours since they had left Scotland.

The only casualty was Bill Carey who had been thrown against the P4 compass which almost tore his knee-cap off. There was no sight of Les Franks. The nose was buried in mud and the remainder of the crew noticed the windscreen on the starboard side was pushed out, and they called out to him:

'Les, where are you?'

From below came the reply, 'Down in the bog!'

He was asked if he was hurt and he called back, 'No, I'm OK, I've landed on my head.'

Gerry chimed in with, 'A bloody good job you did, else you might have got hurt.'

They got Bill Carey out and took him to a nearby wood. Then they tried to set fire to the aircraft but the incendiaries wouldn't work, so they grabbed all the maps, soaked them in petrol and set them alight. The interior of the fuselage caught fire and the aircraft began to burn. The tanks exploded and the ammunition began popping off but the biggest bang came from the exploding oxygen bottles.

On being picked up by the Swedes, they were taken by two men wearing Red Cross arm bands, to a Swedish Army Barracks at Porjus, where they were given a meal. Les Franks asked what it was but Gerry said, 'Shut up and eat.' The commanding officer then said it was cow's lung. With this everyone downed forks in unison and suddenly lost their appetites.

Bill Carey was taken to hospital at Jokkmokk the next day, where he remained until 7th November. He was then taken to Stockholm and remained there until the 23rd when he flew home to England. The remainder of the crew, escorted by a young Swedish army lieutenant, boarded a train for Falun, north-east of Stockholm. They were each given a delicious lunchbox and during the journey, Doug MacLennan burnt their paybooks in the toilet. Midway to Stockholm they were taken to a restaurant and given an excellent meal, which included the rare luxury of ice-cream.

On their arrival in Falun they were taken to a boarding house where they had a steam bath, a swim in a pool and a shower. To their amazement a lady was waiting to towel them dry. Gerry said, 'Cor, they haven't got anything like this in London.'

107

Surprisingly their Lancaster was not completely burnt out and only the forward part was destroyed. An inspection by the Swedish authorities revealed that there was only about 800 litres of petrol left in the tanks. After a time, the engines, fuel tanks and other useful parts were salvaged but to this day the wreck of 'E-Easy' is still in the bog at Porjus. Bill Carey, who came from South Australia, recovered from his injury. He died in a car crash in 1981.

All the other Lancasters returned home. Flying Officer Arthur Kell hung around the target area hoping for a gap in the cloud but eventually he had to set course for base. On arrival at Sumburgh in the Shetlands they were asked if they had bombs on board and they said they had their Tallboy. Kell was ordered to jettison it in the sea but they had no intention of throwing away their valuable cargo, so pretended to drop it and then landed. The people at Sumburgh, on finding the bomb still on board, were not too happy. When Kell was awarded a bar to his DFC in December, mention was made of him landing with his bomb still aboard, despite a damaged hydraulic system!

An air reconnaissance flown later on the 29th gave no satisfactory estimate of any damage to the battleship; it was still on an even keel. Intercepted Norwegian intelligence from radio station Vidar on the 30th, stated a hit on the stern had caused some leaking. In fact the propeller shaft had been damaged by a near miss, causing flooding when 800 tons of water entered the ship. Yet the main fact was undeniable – the *Tirpitz* continued to defy 617's efforts to sink her.

CHAPTER TWELVE

The Sinking

Time and time again the weather had thwarted the crews of 617 Squadron and 9 Squadron in their attempts to sink the mighty battleship *Tirpitz*. Based in the Gulf Stream and with its prevailing westerly wind, Tromso was persistently covered by stratus cloud. The sky was only clear when the wind was easterly.

For the month of November 1944, weathermen expected that only five days might be available for yet another attack on the ship, towards the end of the month. The time limit expired for any daylight attack in 1944 on 26th November. The sun did not rise above the horizon after that date and for a few days there would be only enough twilight to bomb, at mid-day. After that any attack would have to wait until the Spring.

The next attack would be the ninth since March 1942, but if the Allies' peace of mind was to be achieved, the ship had to be destroyed. She had already cost the lives of a number of RAF and FAA aircrew.

On 5th November, there was a false start – again due to weather, fair at first, deteriorating later, but on the 11th the two squadrons again flew to Lossiemouth. On arrival the aircraft were checked over, fuel topped up and the weather confirmed. During the final preparations one of 9 Squadron's ground crew, AC1 Pride, had a lucky escape. As he was priming an engine from inside the starboard wheelwell, in the darkness, the aircraft rolled forward. He just managed to scramble out of the way in time.

There were two WAAFs who knew about the operation before the crews. They were the Williamson twins, Peggy and Joan, both sergeants from Wakefield, Yorkshire. As watch-keepers, they worked in the operations room of the station at Bardney. They, with Sergeant Hilary Anderson, had to sort out the various signals sent from Bomber Command, and pass them on to the various officers to deal with.

At 2.30 a.m. on the 12th, the engines of the Lancasters broke the early morning quiet. Take-off was at 3 a.m. The weather was fine and clear although some icing-up caused last-minute problems to the extent that Wing Commander Jim Bazin, DFC, a former Battle of Britain fighter pilot, now CO of 9 Squadron, did not get off the ground. Squadron Leader Bill Williams, his deputy, was told over the radio after he had become airborne, that he was now in command of the squadron for this operation. The decision to break radio silence to pass on this message was taken by Group Captain McMullen, the overall commander of the raid. Not an easy decision but obviously very vital if there was not to be total confusion over the target. One always had to know who and where the leader is.

All aircraft burned navigation lights to assist the pilots to keep in touch with each other. They headed out at a speed of 185 TAS, the engines set at 1,800 rpm. En route flame flares were dropped for checking drift. By the time the mountains of Norway were crossed it was daylight and large areas of strato-cumulus cloud were depressingly evident. Flying and map reading above the mountains, especially when they are covered by snow and the lakes frozen and snow covered, were tricky. The route had been planned carefully, as there was a gap in the German radar cover in the central part of Norway when aircraft flew below 1,500 feet, due mainly to the mountains. Thus the Lancaster force continued to fly eastwards into Sweden, keeping the mountains between themselves and the known radar stations.

The rendezvous point was Akka Lake, only recognised by a sheet of cloud which covered it, conforming exactly to its shape. The first view of Tromso was without cloud and without smoke. Suddenly, there she was! *Tirpitz* in her anchorage with exactly the conditions they wanted for accurate bombing. As the C-in-C Bomber Command once said, there would be no doubt about the ultimate fate of *Tirpitz*, once the crews were able to draw a bead on her.

The flak thrown up over the ship was plentiful but in the main it was inaccurate. More importantly, there were no fighters. If there had been, havoc would have been played amongst the bombers.

Major Ehrler was still with his JG5 at Bardufoss where they had very recently re-equipped with FW190 fighters. On the morning of the 12th, an alert was sounded in the officers' quarters that several four-engined aircraft in spread formation could be seen above the airfield. Eighteen fighters were 'scrambled' although one 190 was delayed with engine trouble. It appeared, however, that nobody had bothered to tell the German CO that the *Tirpitz* was no longer at Kaa Fjord. His pilots found no Lancasters nor a battleship to defend.

One of the *Tirpitz'* officers, Captain Bernard Schmitz, said, 'We knew well in advance we were to be attacked and we requested the presence of the fighters. The request was granted and the take-off was reported to us. When 28 Lancasters came into sight from the south we enquired as to the whereabouts of our fighters only to discover that they had flown to our old berth at Kaa Fjord and they now did not have enough petrol to return to us and engage the Lancasters.'

Wing Commander Tait, Flying Officers Castagnola and Gingles were the first aircraft to bomb, at 8.41 and 8.42 a.m.; Castagnola claimed a direct hit on the centre of the ship's superstructure. Two crews, those of Flying Officer Ian Ross and Flight Lieutenant Sayers, claimed possible hits on the bows while Flying Officer Flatman reported a direct hit with his bomb behind the funnel which caused flames and a great column of dense, black-reddish smoke. According to the report by Castagnola, there was another direct hit at the same time as his, which, due to the timing, could only have been by Tait or Gingles. The later bomb plots showed Gingles to have scored a near miss so it must be assumed the direct hit was scored by Tait and his crew. Unfortunately the bomb from Willie Tait's aircraft was not plotted, but from the bombing photos taken by his bomb aimer, there is very little doubt that his bomb scored a direct hit. Other direct hits, according to the bomb plot, were scored by F/O Lee, near the ship's aircraft catapult, Flight Lieutenant Anning, near the funnel, and Kell, near the bows.

Flight Lieutenant Keith Aspbury, resting after three operational tours, was working at Air Ministry and having flown on the two previous *Tirpitz* raids, talked Kell into letting him fly in his Lancaster. He had been, when he heard that the third raid was imminent, at Brighton, awaiting a draft back to Australia. On arriving back at Woodhall, he was immediately sent back to Brighton and kept under close watch!

Very near misses were recorded by Ian Ross, Castagnola (although he had claimed a direct hit), Tony Iveson and Flying Officer Leavitt, all of whose bombs fell within 200 feet of the ship. All had bombed between 8.42 and 8.43 a.m. It had been quite an avalanche of Tallboys. 9 Squadron played their part, Flying Officers Tweddle and Newton recording near misses at 8.45. According to Wing Commander Richardson, the Armament Officer at 5 Group, 9 Squadron's plotting indicated large random aiming errors. Bombing by 617 was very concentrated but four bombs dropped at the end of 9 Squadron's attack, fell some 200 yards, 500 yards, ¾ of a mile and one mile, from the ship. In considering the bombing errors, Richardson concluded that only the first 50% of the aircraft to attack would have had a clear or reasonable aiming point and that smoke from explosions must have made subsequent aiming very difficult.

Flying Officer Flatman remembers arriving over the Lake and seeing the others arrive. Wing Commander Tait ordered a Very cartridge to be fired, enabling the others to form a gaggle behind him before pushing on to Tromso. Flatman's bombing run was good and the words 'Bombs gone' by Flying Officer George Kelly, his bomb aimer, were followed by the announcement of a direct hit amidships (later plotted as a near miss). On their return flight a rough engine used more fuel than normal, so they had to land at Scatsta in the Shetlands with only 80 gallons of petrol left.

Flight Sergeant Hibbard, a New Zealander, flew with Flying Officer Joplin, also from New Zealand. Even after all these years he can still see the vivid colours of the prolonged sunrise as they flew between the mountains the entire length of Scandinavia.

Flight Lieutenant Knights remembers his bomb exploding off the port quarter and also seeing one on or near the starboard quarter, starboard bow, port bow and another hit near the funnel. Knights was recommended for an immediate DSO on the 19th, just a week after the attack. He had flown on all three attacks on the *Tirpitz*, the third one being his 67th operation.

Squadron Leader Williams also saw the first 617 bombs go

down, the first falling a little short, the second a very near miss, the third on the island to the left of the ship, the fourth a direct hit amidships.

The first bomb hit the ship just forward of the bridge and put her services out of action. The power of the detonation wave was so great that most of the crew were stunned. The many near misses were recorded, the final one landing about halfway down the length of the hull, detonating right under the ship. It was this bomb that finally turned her over. It caused a 60-foot long dent which was about five feet deep at its centre.

Twenty minutes after the first hit an explosion aboard *Tirpitz* tore a hole 120 feet long on the port side, from deck to keel. A later report by a firm of scrap merchants in Oslo, Hovding Skipsopplugging, put the main damage down to an explosion in the magazine below 'C' turret. The ship very slowly turned turtle to port, rolling through approximately 140°, its superstructure becoming embedded in the sea bottom. Some 85 crewmen were rescued through holes cut in the bottom of the hull within the first 24 hours after the ship turned over. Further rescue attempts were called off after 48 hours. A later inspection of the hull confirmed the following damage: severe damage to the bows, amidships, and a large dent in the propeller shaft housing. The salvage operations showed numerous holes cut in the plates of the ship's side to rescue the survivors that were lucky enough to be able to reach positions of freedom from the steel tomb.

Just before the attack ended, a bomb hit knocked out the gun control position, which accounted for the Lancaster crews reporting a cessation of AA fire from the ship. The Germans found a number of bomb strikes on the land close to the ship; a broken 12,000 lb case was also found on the beach. It had fractured two thirds back from the nose and had probably ricocheted from the ship's side. The broken bomb now resides in a museum in Oslo.

A Norwegian report dated 4th December 1944 listed some of the damage. Serious flooding to the submerged port side; the main mast had been carried away with the result that all the aerials were put out of action. The ship grounded fore and aft and sank amidships into a hollow, which had not been sufficiently filled up, causing the port bilge keel to be carried away. It was thought that considerable changes had occurred in the sea bottom from the effect of the bombs which had fallen away in the vicinity, particularly in the artificial filling of the hollow.

Johannes Ullrich was serving as an observer officer and was based on the highest point of the ship known as the *Vormast*. In the event of an attack this functioned as an artillery command post while at sea. During an air attack or in port the artillery command post was in the region of the ship's bridge. Ullrich recalls:

'On the morning of the 12th we were in the mess having breakfast, when the first reports of English planes from South Norway were reported. Later followed the order – "All anti-aircraft crews to their guns." This, as far as I can remember, was about 9 a.m.

'I stood by one of the large E-Mess-Units in the *Vormast* and scanned the sky for enemy aircraft. The Captain said, "We can certainly rely on protection from the fighters at Bardufoss." Towards 9.30 the bombers first came into view, visibility was good and they could be seen from about fifty kilometres away. They were flying on a parallel course to the ship, and we, at first, thought that the attack was not intended for us, but then a group of twenty-five aircraft veered towards us. The heavy artillery opened fire from a range of about twenty-five kilometres. This didn't stop them. Firing was then commenced from the lighter guns resulting in hellish noise and smoke.

'We saw that the aircraft only carried one bomb of a large size, observed their release and saw them coming towards us. The first hits rocked the ship sideways and she listed slightly. As I looked out on the water, some sailors had already jumped in, simply because they could not hold on because of the angle of the ship's list.

'Then came the order from the Captain: "Save yourself if you can." We stood at the railings and looked at the deep water below us, a distance of 20-25 metres. I jumped into the water in full uniform but without a lifebelt, entered the water and in the excitement I did not even feel the intense cold of the sea. Before jumping I had looked at my watch, it was 9.47. I swam away from the ship as quickly as I could when suddenly there was an explosion and the roof of the gun turret disintegrated like paper in the air.

The ship made a last movement and turned turtle, which resulted in a huge flood wave.'

Leutnant Fassender was also on the ship at the time and remembered the visibility being good and that '... wireless transmission signals reported one Lancaster in the Bodo area at 8.15 and three were reported at Mosjoen, course east. At 8.25 another four Lancasters were reported at Mosjoen, course east. At 8.25 another four Lancasters were reported in the same area. Fighter protection was requested from Bardufoss at 8.55 a.m. An airfield alert was given at 9.02 and the ship cleared for action at 9.05, on the sighting of an open formation of about twenty to twenty-five aircraft, seventy-five miles to the south. Fighter protection was still being requested at 9.15, but a broadcast from the base at Bardufoss said that an enemy formation was over Bardufoss and it was impossible to take off.

'At 9.25 one fighter was reported as taking off; shortly afterwards further fighters were reported to have taken off. At 9.27, the Captain broadcast to the ship's company: "We are expecting a heavy air attack. The ship's company of *Tirpitz* will fulfil its duty again this time and prepare a hot reception for the four-engined bombers." Smoke flares sighted from first formation about twenty-five miles away, time 9.38. At 9.40 the Captain gave an order to the senior gunnery officer, "Open fire when bombers are within range." The forward main armament opened fire when the formation was thirteen miles away, and the secondary armament and heavy anti-aircraft opened fire when the formation was about nine miles, time 9.42. A stick of heavy calibre bombs fell from close proximity mostly inside the net the ship was enclosed in.

'Two direct hits were observed on the port side, one on the aircraft's catapult and one abreast of 'B' gun turret. The ship flooded with the high water columns from the explosions and it later listed heavily to port, time 9.45. At 9.50 with a list of 30 to 40 degrees, an order came from the Captain to abandon lower decks. At 9.52, now with a list of 60-70 degrees, 'C' turret went up in flames, then the ship capsized to port and was lying at an angle.'

Eyewitness accounts from Norway were plentiful, such as Helge Richardson of Tromso. 'I lived at Bjerkaker, near the south end of Tromso island. As a hobby I ran a little mink farm just outside my house. I was feeding the animals early on the morning of Sunday, 12th November, when the German batteries opened fire. From the direction of Balsfjord came the English aircraft towards *Tirpitz*, which was anchored at the end of Haakoy, a few kilometres from Tromso.

'This time the *Tirpitz* was hit and in a short while only the bottom of the ship could be seen. In my opinion the defence from the ship was not as good as one would expect from such a ship. All the aircraft turned south in the main but a few went to the north again to inspect the damage. It was the happiest day in Tromso.

'Later, when business friends' children came from other countries and asked for possible souvenirs from the ship, we searched for bomb splinters and found many for them.'

Jons Olsen was out with a fishing vessel at the time and recalls: 'We arrived at Tromso on the night of the 11th. On Sunday the 12th, we went to an oil tank to fill up when a German came running down warning us away shouting of an air warning. We then went south near the *Tirpitz*. As no aeroplanes were seen I started to fill up with oil, but then the crew of the ship shouted they could hear aircraft. On hearing this I slowed up and stayed in the area.

'I then saw a formation of aircraft, as far as I can remember, coming from the mainland. The Germans opened up with everything they had, but the aircraft broke formation and flew in one by one over the ship, dropping their bombs. After the first bomb had dropped nothing more of the ship was seen because of the smoke and vapour. When the last bomb had been dropped, a powerful explosion occurred and fire and vapour rose to a height of 300 metres. The weather was quite calm and sunny at the time. It must have been a reflection of the sun as the sun does not rise at that time of the year until about noon.

'When the vapour had faded away we saw the battleship had turned on her side.'

Mr Egil Akre, from Oslo, was arrested in the spring of 1944 by German police and sent to nortꞏern Norway. Early in November, the Norwegian prisoners were set free, given a little money and told to make their own way southwards:

'I came to Tromso the day before the attack and rented a room at Jenson's Hotel. The next day, I was up early to check on transport

116

to Oslo, when I heard an air raid warning being sounded. I ran from the hotel, which lay close to the harbour, and up the hill above Tromso. I got so far across the hill and I could see the *Tirpitz*. As yet there were no sounds of aircraft, or any shooting, then suddenly the sound of engines in the sky, and the shore batteries opening up. A man came out of one of the houses and invited me to take cover in his cellar. We stood watching the attack through the cellar window and saw hits on the deck of the ship and the final hit on the ammunition chambers which set off a violent explosion. The ship very slowly started to turn over and ended up with most of the bottom of its hull visible. Many men were jumping into the water and the ship and oil around the ship was on fire.

'On the way back to Tromso I went through a wood, where the ship could not be seen and met fifteen to twenty sailors from the ship, some in uniform and others in training clothes. They carried a net full of footballs and looked completely unconcerned. I said, "*Tirpitz ist versunken*" [*Tirpitz* has been sunk.] One of them pointed and said to the others, "*Verrückter Norweger.*" [crazy Norwegian].'

Mrs Thordis Ryeng, now seventy-nine years old, was one of the few people living in Naakoy at the time. Her husband and seven children made a living out of farming and fishing. With the arrival of *Tirpitz* their little place was transformed into a war theatre; flak batteries arrived and Germans were everywhere. Several of the nearby farms were commandeered by the Germans. On the second Saturday after the *Tirpitz* arrived, they received a visit from a young German who spoke excellent Norwegian. Mrs Ryeng could not resist teasing him by saying, 'Tomorrow the English will come and bomb the *Tirpitz* to pieces.' He laughed and replied, '*Tirpitz* is like a fortress, and nobody would be able to finish her off.'

A week passed and the situation was strained with the children staying in the bunkers all day, and only coming into the house to eat and sleep. A little later her son, Vida, came running in and said, '*Tirpitz* has swung out her guns.'

'I glanced out of the window to see *Tirpitz* fire her first salvo. I could then see the aircraft approaching over the mountains, so I opened the doors and windows and left the house and sought shelter in the barn while the bombing went on.

'The cows crouched in their stalls and the wall of the barn moved

117

like a ship on the water in a stormy sea. When it stopped we went outside to see what had happened. At first we saw nothing but smoke, but heard many screams and shouts from people in the most terrible pain. Two words were screamed over and over again, "*Mutter*" and "*Hilfe*". [Mother and Help]. The ship was covered by smoke and the water seemed to be burning, and in this inferno men were swimming.

'As the smoke began to lift and we could see better, we saw several boats and launches. Suddenly we noticed *Tirpitz* lying there with her bottom pointing to the sky. It looked like a silver island. About a week later the German speaking Norwegian returned. He was a changed man, broken by the loss of his friends. The next day after the attack he had rowed out to the ship and saw men trying to get the trapped sailors out of the ship. After a week or so noises were still heard coming from the ship in the form of morse signals.'

Just prior to the attack, the Germans had delivered hundreds of smoke canisters to Haakoy and had in fact started constructing gun emplacements on the mountains, but the attack was made before these positions were fully prepared. To this day you can still see these canisters and the remains of gun emplacements.

Mr Leif Erik Simonson had his house taken over by the Germans – Naval officers from *Tirpitz*. After he had seen the ship roll over he ran home full of joy to tell his parents, but was arrested by one of the Naval officers. His father later told him the Germans were going to shoot him and only his age saved him – he was fifteen. He heard of many stories of the men trapped in the hull. Two were kept alive by drinking alcohol. When they were found they were in the ship's wine cellars.

Lars Thoring lived in Tromso at the time of the attack, and was later the town clerk. He remembers that during the attack windows shattered and wall pictures fell from their hooks. Also that although the ship's guns were silenced, an anti-aircraft unit on Haakoy continued to fire and worry the attacking aircraft. One Tallboy fell on or near the battery and it was silenced; the crater can still be seen to this day.

In order to have a better view, Thoring climbed up an observation platform (or weather station), but he was ordered down by a German officer when the attack started. Photographs, however, were taken from the platform during the attack.

Emil Olson and Jak Jakobson observed the bombing of the *Tirpitz* through a telescope and could see the water being pushed away by the bombs exploding around the ship, so the bottom occasionally looked like a dry beach. This, in their opinion, contributed to the battleship heeling over.

Kaare Johnson also thought that the ship went over because both the sand and water had been blown away on one side of the ship. Wounded German sailors were swimming in the sea crying for help, and he saw several Germans crawling on the bottom of the ship and a few clinging to the anti-torpedo nets. The Germans worked all night to get the men out of the ship, cutting holes in the hull. A while later he witnessed Germans parading, many with bandages. They were from *Tirpitz* and were going back to Germany. There were about eighty out of a crew of some 1,800 from the ship. A boy called Simonson was nicknamed 'Von Tirpitz' after he had clapped his hands while watching the *Tirpitz* roll over and had been arrested. A message was sent to England that the *Tirpitz* was lost. The radio operator had a secret room in the local hospital and he had seen the first wounded being brought in.

Immediately after the sinking members of the Luftwaffe, anti-aircraft units, signals units and the German Navy at Oslo were brought before a military court. The Luftwaffe Gruppe Commander, Major Ehrler, received three years' hard labour, which meant solitary confinement. Ten officers from the anti-aircraft unit were jailed. In the event, Ehrler did not serve his sentence but went on flying until 4th April 1945. On this date he was killed flying a Messerschmitt 262 jet fighter, shot down by an American Mustang over Berlin.

Three reasons could be given for the breakdown in communication by the German defences:

1. No warning of the approaching British aircraft.
2. Lack of combat orders and air protection for the ship.
3. Difficulty in operations from Bardufoss, compounded by the unit there changing their aircraft.

As already related, the Gruppe Commander was sentenced to three years in prison, and held responsible for *Tirpitz* being lost. After four weeks the sentence was waived and he was posted to JG7.

He had been nominated for the Crossed Swords to his Knight's Cross but never received this decoration. At twenty eight years of age he was a broken man.

The defences only damaged one Lancaster sufficiently for it to be unable to return home. The aircraft, of 9 Squadron, crash-landed in Sweden, just as the 617 aircraft had done on the previous attack. The photograph of their attack on the ship was recovered, developed, and is now in the UK. The aircraft wreck still lies as it crashed that November day.

The report from the photographic Lancaster of 463 Squadron (PD329) which accompanied the attack force, and had been on the previous two attacks, was of interest. The crew were all Australian, except for Flight Lieutenant Sinclair, who came from Dundee in Scotland. The pilot was Flight Lieutenant Bruce Buckham, who came from Sydney. Their take-off had been delayed because of heavy frosting on the aircraft, but they finally got away and saw the attack very clearly, observing excellent attacks on the ship's stern and bows.

Early bombs, according to their report, slightly overshot, but approximately the fourth bomb was a direct hit amidships. As the attack developed more hits were recorded on the stern, amidships and finally on the bows until the ship was unable to fire her own guns. There were also several near misses. Suddenly, after the attack had ended, the ship was seen to heel over towards the island and become half submerged.

Flight Lieutenant Buckham said, 'We knew a lot of damage had been done because we could see more than the attacking crews, but I could still see her afloat and thought, she's never going to sink. I had actually set a course for home when my rear gunner, who was actually a cameraman on this trip, came up and said, "I think she is going to heel over." I swung the aircraft round and looked again. *Tirpitz* was listing over at an angle of 70-80°. You could see the keel painted red, glistening in the sunlight. I thought it was worth while going around again, so we made another run and got a grand picture at about 5,000 feet.'

Part of this film, after security clearance, was given world-wide release in the newsreels in Britain, the Commonwealth and the

120

USA. The film now resides in the Imperial War Museum in London.

Flight Lieutenant Buckham and his crew returned to Waddington after a journey of 14 hours, 19 minutes, and he received an immediate DSO for his work. His crew were also decorated, DFCs going to Flying Officer Proctor, Flight Lieutenant Giersch (he was in the rear turret), Pilot Officer Manning, Pilot Officer Holder, the wireless operator, while the navigator, Flying Officer Board, DFC, received a bar to his decoration.

The interpretation report, dated 21st November, based on an analysis of the film and the bombing photographs, showed a direct hit near the port end of the ship's catapult. A second bomb fell in the water, followed, by an interval of about one second, by a bomb burst on the southern tip of the island, and an $\frac{1}{8}$th of a second later a brilliant flash of light followed by an explosion in the sea on the port side in the region of the after range finder. This was bomb number four, number five fell inside the boom off the port side. Number six fell between the boom and the shore, then number seven fell inside the boom off the starboard side, while number eight fell near to where number six had fallen.

During the interval between the falling of bombs eight and nine, the photographs showed the ship plunge to starboard. It was estimated she was displaced by about 12 feet. Bomb number eight was followed, about $1\frac{1}{2}$ seconds later, by number nine, which made a near miss off the port quarter, close to 'Y' turret. This burst quickly developed into a high column of heavy black smoke, and $1\frac{1}{2}$ seconds later a bright flash was observed midships which was not a bomb burst, but may well have been exploding ammunition. Some time after number nine had fallen, a light-coloured jet was seen rising from the sea amidships. A burst boiler or the in-rush of sea water into the boiler room would probably produce a similar result. Bomb number ten fell close in shore and a great disturbance of water was observed between the ship and the shore.

Bombs eleven, twelve and thirteen fell in the water at least 1,000 feet to the east of the ship, number fourteen falling close to the stern. Number fifteen fell in-shore on the east side of Haakoy island, and number sixteen slightly south of bomb number twelve.

Photographs were taken by a Mosquito some hours later which showed *Tirpitz* completely capsized with an estimated 720 feet of keel exposed. She was lying in nine fathoms of water. It is now known that by 11.30 p.m. on the 12th, 596 survivors had been rescued, but the loss of life was high. It was also evident that salvage of the ship was hopeless. A radio message from Radio Station Vidar (in the Tromso area) on the 12th, confirmed, '*Tirpitz* capsized after a series of hits. A little of the ship's keel is above water.'

Thus ended the life of the battleship *Tirpitz*, just four years and two days after she had been completed. Through the whole of her career she neither sank nor damaged a single Allied ship. Her only achievement was in pinning down important British Naval forces during critical periods of the war when they could have usefully been employed elsewhere. She had been attacked by the Navy, the Fleet Air Arm and the RAF, cost many Allied lives, but finally died under a hail of bombs by 9 and 617 Squadrons, RAF.

Wing Commander Willie Tait flew to London on the 14th to make a broadcast about the attack. He returned the next day to meet the Secretary of State for Air, Sir Archibald Sinclair, who visited Woodall Spa. Sir Archibald wanted to express his admiration of the magnificent exploit of sinking *Tirpitz*, saying that he spoke on behalf of the Government, the Air Council and with the feelings of all their fellow countrymen in thanking them.

'The people of this country will take great pride in the destruction of the *Tirpitz* as an achievement of British aircraft, manned by British crews, working on a British bombsight and dropping British bombs which no other air force in the world today can carry, except the Royal Air Force. It is an astonishing development that has taken place during these five years of war in air power. If you look back at the beginning of the war, and now, in November 1944, you can carry a 12,000 pound bomb a distance of 1,200 miles to Tromso and 1,200 miles back, drop a bomb when you get there from 16,000 to 17,000 feet with an accuracy which could have been undreamed of four to five years ago, even from a very low height.

'Much of this achievement must be owed to ground staff. The planning staff arrangements, the servicing of aircraft and the efficiency of the ground crews as well as our splendid air crews. Gentlemen, we have sunk the toughest ship in the world and I'm sure, in the war. You are now going on forty-eight hours leave; go home and tell your story, your people at home have had a hard time during this war, a lot of troubles, losses, suffering. Thank you all for all you have achieved in the sinking of *Tirpitz* and good luck to you in the hard fighting which yet lies ahead.'

Squadron Leader Williams of 9 Squadron also went to London for a press conference at the Ministry of Information. In the evening he made a broadcast with Ed Morrow to the USA. Newspapers printed headlines of the victory. The *News Chronicle* had – 'The *Tirpitz* is Sunk. 12,000 lbs send her to the bottom of Tromso Fiord.' *Daily Express* – 'Unsinkable sunk upside down. 700 feet showing. Three quake bombs hit, and she capsizes.'

Many messages of congratulations were received. The King sent one on the 14th, which read: 'Please convey my hearty congratulations to all those who took part in the daring and successful attack on *Tirpitz*.' From the President of the USA, dated 13th: 'Death of the *Tirpitz* is great news. We must help the Germans by never letting them build anything like it again, thus putting the German Treasury on its feet.' – Roosevelt. Barnes Wallis sent a message to the AOC of 5 Group: 'Very hearty congratulations to you and all officers and crews of 617 Squadron on the magnificent success achieved yesterday. The tremendous courage and skill displayed has resulted in a major victory for Bomber Command.'

The C-in-C Bomber Command sent a message to Wallis in reply, 'Many thanks for your message. On the contrary, success entirely due to your perseverance with your bomb.' Winston Churchill wrote: 'Congratulations to all', while Stalin's message to Churchill read, 'The news that British aeroplanes have sunk the *Tirpitz* has greatly delighted us. British airmen may legitimately pride themselves on this deed.'

Awards were recommended for the operation. The DSO went to Bobby Knights, as already mentioned, and the DFC to Pilot Officer Norman Evans, who had been Castagnola's bomb aimer, and on his 42nd trip. On the 21st Willie Tait was recommended for the

Victoria Cross. He had now flown 98 operations and already had a DSO and two bars and a DFC and bar. He had joined his first squadron in April 1940 and completed thirty trips in four months. He later commanded No 10 Squadron and then 78 Squadron; then he was promoted to group captain, a rank he, like Cheshire, had relinquished in order to command 617 and fly on operations once more. He was not awarded a VC but given a third bar to his DSO. He completed two more trips with 617 to bring his total ops to 100 then left the squadron to take up a post at No 100 Group.

In September 1945 Tait visited *Tirpitz*, flying there in a Sunderland flying boat from the Shetland Islands. The hulk was red with rust. A ghastly smell seeped from the rotting hull; nearly 1,000 bodies were still inside it, while oil continued to leak from her. In May 1945, Air Commodore Bilney, Bomber Command's Armaments Officer flew to Tromso to inspect the results of the attack at first hand.

Squadron Leader Bill Williams' wife went into a shop and asked for a bottle of sherry which at the time was in short supply. The man in the shop recognised her from a photograph taken with Bill that their local paper had printed and said she could have two bottles!

In 1946, Bjorn Rosenerger, then sixteen years old, rowed out to the ship. It rose above the water like a shiny cliff. He walked along the hull and where the rescue teams had broken through to the bulkheads was a fantastic sight. They were painted white. On the eastern one was a mural of *Tirpitz* at full speed with the words '*Gegen Engeland*'. He later discovered that it was removed and donated to the squadron which sank her. This part of the bulkhead was in fact presented to Bomber Command in February 1950. It came from Tromso on HM Fishery Protectorate Vessel *Mariner* and was collected at Chatham Docks on 1st December 1949. It measured three feet by four feet six inches, and weighed 2 cwt. It was presented to 617 Squadron and 9 Squadron at Binbrook later in 1950. Over the years it became the practice of the two squadrons to steal it from each other but it now resides at the new museum at Hendon, north London.

Another souvenir was presented to a member of 617. Part of the upper deck was sent to Captain Hubert C. Knilans, DSO, DFC in the USA in June 1949. Nick of course, had taken part in the first operation against *Tirpitz* via Russia.

On the north-east side of Tromso lie heaps of rusty torpedo netting which had surrounded the ship. When the ship was cut up after the war, all the upper steel was removed leaving just the hulk 12 metres below the surface. Nothing can now be seen from the shore. The teak deck was taken ashore and used on a quay on the west side of Tromso, but this has since been removed. An electric motor was taken to Hommingsvag in the county of Finnmark and used to produce electric power during the re-building of the village there after the war. It produced 500 kilowatts and to this day it is still there as a spare power supply. A good many boiler pipes were taken ashore and used as posts for people's gardens.

Salvage work on the ship was a dangerous and formidable task. She was full of oil and several fires were started while work went on, one so bad that the whole project was nearly abandoned. Great masses of steel and iron were melted down for nails and screws. Most of the engines were undamaged and miles of electric cable and steam pipes were salvaged. Parts of the top mast made a toy horse for the children of Haakoy.

The salvage workers lived on board small steamers and were given free board and lodgings as well as beer. When the ship was being broken up, some of the macabre moments of the last hour of its life were discovered. On cutting through a crumpled bulkhead a skeleton of a trapped ship's fireman was discovered in the last moments of life, still clutching a pipe in his boney fingers.

In a broadcast from Tromso on 8th July 1949, and a BBC TV programme of 20th November, details of the ship were revealed. One of the most active men in the Resistance in Tromso was a radio operator, Egil Linberg. With his portable equipment he watched movement of the ship and signalled London as to her position. The Germans tried to detect his signals to locate his position and he had many a narrow escape. After the war his health deteriorated; he developed a heart disease and died in 1952 when only forty-two years old, leaving a widow and son.

CHAPTER THIRTEEN

A New Era

The outstanding month of November also brought the usual crop of postings in and out of the squadron. Pilots posted in were Flight Lieutenants Brookes, Gavin, Lancey, Horsley, Squadron Leader Calder and Flying Officer Lee.

Robert Horsley had previously been a wireless operator with 50 Squadron, and been in the crew of Pilot Officer Leslie Thomas Manser. They were part of the force of over 1,000 bombers which flew to Cologne on the night of 30/31st May 1942 – the first thousand bomber raid. On the way to the target, their Manchester aircraft was hit by flak, but Manser completed their bomb run before turning for home. Hit again and then with one engine on fire and with a wounded rear gunner aboard, he ordered his crew to bale out. Keeping the aircraft in the air while they did so, he sacrified his own life, his reward being a posthumous Victoria Cross. Horsley received the DFC,[1] later became a pilot, and was now a member of 617.

The squadron's first operation after sinking the *Tirpitz* was on 8th December. The previous day, advancing American troops were preparing to cross the River Roer. At the head of the Roer valley was the Urft Dam, which retained an immense volume of water. It was feared the Germans would release the water while the Americans were in the act of crossing the river, for they were only three miles away from the dam. If the dam could be burst before the crossing commenced, the water would have subsided by the time the crossing took place. It was another Kembs Dam operation.

So, on the morning of the 8th, nineteen Avro Lancasters climbed into the sky, and headed for the Roer valley. Over the target, their

[1] For escaping back to the U.K.

old enemy – cloud – caused the operation to be abandoned despite several attempts to make run-ins.

Flying Officer Jones, in Squadron Leader Brookes' crew, remembers them going down low to have a close look at Dunkirk on the way back. They flew over the town at a height of about 300 feet, whereupon every gun in the town opened fire. They had not realised the town was still in German hands. Luckily some of the flak bounced off the bomb beneath the aircraft! They landed at an American base at Sudbury. On arrival they requested permission to drop the Tallboy on the grass to save further damage to the aircraft but this was vigorously turned down by the American base commander. To get the bomb back to Woodhall it was necessary for a bomb trolley to be sent to Sudbury, as the Americans had no equipment large enough to cope with it.

To add more difficulty to an already bad day, 617 found thick fog when they returned and had to be diverted to Manston, landing with the aid of FIDO – a runway lit with burning petrol which dispersed the fog.

Another attack on the dam was arranged for the 11th, this time with seventeen aircraft. Take-off came at lunch-time and this time they were able to bomb successfully and hits were seen on the dam. Three notable failures were those of Squadron Leader Cockshott, despite five runs impeded each time by cloud, and Flight Lieutenant Gavin who had a partial hang-up and had to release the bomb manually, causing an overshoot. Flying Officer Sanders made six runs but smoke and cloud obscured the aiming point. Damage assessment showed 13 feet of the top of the dam broken away, but the Germans succeeded in preventing further erosion of the dam wall by manipulating the water level.

On the 15th it was back to U-Boat pen targets again – and again those at the base at Ijmuiden were the target. Fighter cover for the seventeen Lancasters was provided by 11 Group; Tait led 617. Flak over the target was quite heavy, but the Lancasters flew in and dropped their Tallboys. Tait saw his bomb fall on the south pens near the centre. Brookes had a hang-up, the gyro having toppled giving the impression the bomb had gone. He then circled south-west of the target for fifteen minutes waiting for the gyro to settle down, but it didn't and he was ordered home. As he tried to re-cock the bomb, it slipped and fell into the sea.

Calder was hit by light flak which damaged the Lancaster's main spar, and the machines of Flight Lieutenant Pryor and Marshall were also hit. Marshall in fact brought his bomb back having had his starboard inner engine made useless and set on fire. He put the Lancaster into a dive and pressed the extinguisher, putting the fire out. Despite three bombing runs the bomb failed to release. When he landed at Woodhall the bomb fell off at dispersal, and the crew made a very hasty exit from the aeroplane! Flying Officer Flatman also had a hang-up after making two runs. As he turned for the third he opened the bomb doors about two miles out and the bomb fell out.

Flying Officer Watts' machine also caught some flak in the front turret, and his windscreen was shattered on the port side. The bomb aimer's vision was obscured by oil pouring from various fractured pipe lines. The base of a shell, about the size of a tea-plate and quite a bit thicker, went into the front turret occupied by Flying Officer Jewell. He was very lucky as it missed his head by no more than an inch.

Damage photos and reports from Ijmuiden showed part of the roof over four of the entrances to the pens, measuring 120 feet, had collapsed and another hit had made a hole in the roof about 15 feet across.

A long range operation was laid on for 21st December; the target was the synthetic oil plant at Politz near Stettin, in the far east of Germany. The weather on take-off for the sixteen Lancasters was filthy, with visibility down to just a few yards. The operation had already been postponed once that day at the last moment, and the crews had had to sit in the aircraft to await a new take-off time. On arrival over the target the bombing seemed to be very scattered. Most of the bombs appeared to be falling north of the plant. Flying Officer Watts' bomb sight became useless ten minutes before reaching the target. Owing to the close proximity of a POW camp the crews had been warned at briefing about the danger of indiscriminate bombing, so they and Flight Lieutenant Marshall and his crew brought their bombs home.

Squadron Leader Cockshott made three runs but could not see

the target. On his fourth attempt the bombing gyro toppled but his man in the nose still bombed at 10.10 p.m. Tony Iveson also had his bomb sight gyro topple on his first run and, following further attempts, he too brought his bomb home. Squadron Leader Brookes had his aircraft hit by heavy flak which damaged the underside of the bomber, including the bomb doors, preventing him from dropping his bomb.

A general comment from the captains and bomb aimers who bombed visually was that the target was clearly visible in the light of the flares but on the other hand the construction of the target did not provide a really distinct aiming point which was so essential for the SABS bomb sight. It was concluded that at least three Tallboys fell in the target area.

Flying Officer Joplin (in ME561 'T') was hit by flak and set course for home. On approaching base at Woodall, fog covered the base and it was obvious that landing would be difficult. Joplin decided to make for Ludford Magna which was equipped with FIDO. When Joplin called Ludford Magna on the radio he found the sky was full of other aircraft also seeking permission to land.

By now his fuel was very low and the flight engineer didn't think they could make Scotland, where visibility was reported to be better. They then received a radio message instructing them to return directly to Ludford Magna. Shortly before they sighted the FIDO through the clouds, Joplin decided to land but during the approach there was a tremendous bang. The light went out and the aircraft shot up into the air – the port wing had hit the ground. The needles of the engine gauges were doing a dance, completely haywire. Frank Tilley, the engineer, pushed the throttles forward 'through the gate' to give maximum revs. to the engines, in an attempt to gain height but all to no avail. Joplin was calling on the radio, 'T-Tommy crashing,' again and again, as he ordered the crew into crash positions. Seconds later they hit.

On impact the rear turret broke away. They had crashed on farm land near Market Rason at 2.45 a.m. Frank Tilley had his leg broken and crawled away from the now blazing wreck. Basil Fish, the navigator, was knocked unconscious but soon came round, with Tilley shouting for him to get out of the aircraft. This he did, staggering out to be immediately ill. He then went back and

129

dragged Joplin out, and then Gordon Cooke. Joplin had multiple fractures of both legs and to this day walks with a limp. Cooke had the tendons of his wrist burnt through and some internal injuries, while the rear gunner, James Thompson, suffered severe back injuries. Fish returned to the aircraft, where by now the heat was intense and burning ammunition exploding in all directions. He saw a body on the floor of the aircraft but was unable to get to it because of the heat. He thought it was Bob Yates, the mid-upper, who had been thrown forward with the bomb aimer, Flying Officer Arthur Walker, shortly before the crash.

Fish set off to seek help but suddenly realised he was himself bleeding heavily from the head. He crawled through ploughed fields and hedges in dense fog and finally came across a remote farm and woke the farmer. He proved to be most helpful and directed him to a telephone box from where he was able to contact the nearest RAF station which sent out a rescue team who managed to locate the crash site. The injured were taken to Lough County Infirmary, a civilian hospital, and later to RAF Rauch military hospital.

Frank Tilley remembers spending a week in the crash ward and seeing how badly injured others were in the ward from other crashed aircraft. When he was able to get about, with a leg in plaster, he was picked up at the hospital by the Red Cross, who took him by train to London, and from the station to his home in North London.

Arthur Walker and Bob Yates were killed. Walker, not a regular member of the crew, had taken the place of Loftus Hebbard who had been taken into hospital with tonsilitis on the 20th. Walker had just returned from leave to be told he had still two ops. to do before completing his second tour of operations. He already had a DFC from his first tour and was twenty-two years old.

His regular pilot in 617 had been Bobby Knights who remembers him as a most reliable and efficient bomb-aimer and crew member. Knights felt it a great tragedy that he did not finish his second tour with him after the final *Tirpitz* attack.

On 28th December 1944, Wing Commander J.B. 'Willie' Tait, received the third bar to his Distinguished Service Order. This was unique to the RAF at that time. The award coincided with his leaving 617 Squadron. At a farewell party, the new CO was present, Group Captain J.E. 'Johnnie' Fauquier, DSO, DFC, a 35-year-old Canadian, from Ottowa. Pre-war he had flown more than 3,000 hours as a commercial airways pilot before joining the RCAF in 1939. Posted to 405 Canadian Squadron in 1941, he had risen to wing commander rank by 1942, to command the squadron. In 1943 he was promoted to group captain and took part in the famous Peenemünde raid, acting as deputy marker to Group Captain John Searby of 83 Squadron. On this raid he made seventeen passes over the target, remaining in the area for forty-five minutes during which time he saw twenty-five shot down. For his part in the attack he received an immediate DSO by Air Commodore Don Bennett, who commanded the Pathfinder Force. It was Fauquier's 36th op.

In March 1944 he was awarded a bar to his DSO on completion of his second bomber tour, was promoted to air commodore, but reverted back to group captain so he could begin a third tour as CO of 617 Squadron. In April 1945 he won a second bar to his DSO, the first Canadian officer to be so decorated. He had also received the DFC, French Croix de Guerre and Legion of Honour. In 1973 he was made a member of the Canadian Aviation Hall of Fame. He died in 1981 and was buried in Toronto. His last request was that he be buried in his blazer with the 617 Squadron badge on the pocket. Six pall bearers and a Guard of Honour were sent by the Commanding Officer of the Canadian Forces Base in Toronto. A firing party and a Canadian Forces padre were also at the graveside at Beechwood Cemetery, Toronto.

The last three days of 1944 saw three operations by the squadron, to end a momentous year. On the 29th, 617 went for the E-Boat pens in Rotterdam. Sixteen Lancasters carried Tallboys set with 16-second fuses. The pens were situated at the east side of the Waalhaven; three sections with a total of 16 pens each. The dimensions of each pen were 150 feet by 25 feet and the roof had been camouflaged to make it look like a green hill. There were some gun positions on the roof.

It was a very successful attack with several hits being scored, three being direct hits on the southern portion of the shelter. A crater some 25 feet in diameter was made on the entrance of the southern shelter roof and a small building was destroyed. In addition a great length of roof over the entrance, measuring 188 by 20 feet in length and width was smashed. Two out of three sections of the shelter were damaged, the centre one collecting a direct hit on the roof which destroyed two buildings over the shelter entrance. There was also heavy damage which caused the collapse of the roof 118 feet in length and 38 feet in width. Other bombs which fell near some barrack type building and stores, destroyed or severely damaged a number of buildings, whilst the quayside lost some 400 feet. Nearby railways tracks were cut in a number of places.

On the 30th, 617 once again returned to the U-boat pens at Ijmuiden, an attack for which thirteen aircraft were assigned. Over the target at 6,000 feet, 10/10ths cloud was encountered. Squadron Leader Calder, who went down to 4,000 feet just out from the target, found more low cloud covering the target area. He had little option than to call off the raid.

On New Year's Eve, shipping in Oslo Fjord attracted the attention of 617's aircraft and bombs; Fauquier led a force of twelve Lancasters. So there was no New Year's Party unless it was to be held over a hostile target, as the drop time was set for around midnight. The targets were the German cruisers *Köln* and *Emden*. As in past night ops, the crews bombed by the light of flares but these fell too far to the north of the ships. When directed by Fauquier to drop others further south, they were over-corrected and 617 ended up by bombing by the light of the moon.

Fauquier's bomb aimer let their bomb go from 8,000 feet and it burst about 100 yards on the port side of the *Köln* and the ship made off at high speed in a northerly direction. Flight Lieutenant Pryor made six runs but his bomb aimer could not see the targets and did not bomb, and nor did Flatman as he found the conditions over the area too murky. By now both ships were on the move, at a speed judged to be about 30 knots, while their gunners sent up quite a defensive fire. However, despite no success, all aircraft safely returned to base. It was later reported, that a near miss on a large ship by a Tallboy, swung her 90° to starboard and brought her to a standstill.

So ended 1944. Would 1945 see victory? Although the net

132

seemed to be closing in around Hitler's Reich, the Battle of the Ardennes, the German offensive that had taken the Allies by surprise was in full swing, and on the morning of 1st January 1945, the German Luftwaffe tried desperately to knock out elements of the Allied Tactical Air Forces in Holland and France. The struggle seemed to be far from ending.

CHAPTER FOURTEEN

Touch and Go

A trip to Bergen on 12th January 1945, seemed, with a fighter escort, to be one of 617's easier operations. However, because of a communication problem with the escort, this was far from the case. The operation was to attack shipping and the U-Boat pens at Bergen. Three aircraft were detailed to select a ship and were armed with Tallboy bombs, all of which had 5-second fuses. They were to attack in such a way that if they overshot the target, the bomb would fall in either open water or on barren land. No ship was to be attacked within 150 yards of a quay or built-up area. A further three with 5-second fused Tallboys were to attack a floating dock in which there was a submarine, while the remaining eleven Lancasters were to bomb the pens with 11-second fused Tallboys.

Flying with them was 9 Squadron, which was still the only other RAF squadron able to carry the Tallboys. Their brief was to select a suitable aiming point off the target and to estimate wind vectors. 617 was to bomb direct with their SABS while 9 Squadron used their Mark 14 sights.

The total of thirty-one aircraft from the two squadrons were to be escorted by 13 Group Mustangs – 315 Polish Squadron, led by Squadron Leader Tadeusz Andersz. Johnnie Fauquier led 617 in a Mosquito (NT205). The escort was due to pick up the bombers off Peterhead, and two Warwick aircraft from Fraserburgh were to act in an air-sea-rescue role if required. They would patrol off the target area until the Lancasters had left. To complete the force, there were two Mosquitos of 141 Squadron (No 100 Group) also forming part of the escort.

The weather was clear midway across the North Sea to the target, but a smoke screen in the vicinity of the pens, plus a ground haze, made target identification difficult, resulting in the bombers spending about three quarters of an hour in the target area. Flak was at first moderate but became more accurate as the attack went on. Some twenty Focke Wulf 190s and Messerschmitt 109s were airborne during the attack, the 190s coming from Herdla, a base twenty miles to the north-west of Bergen, and a number of combats took place.

Air raid warnings were sounded in Bergen at 12.52 p.m., as the Lancasters with their escort were observed from the ground. Jan Hjornevik, aged seventeen, lived in a house on a mountain side and attended school in Bergen. He was on his way to school when suddenly anti-aircraft guns opened fire, and he saw British aircraft approaching across the sea from the north. They were easy to spot as the sun was reflecting on their cockpits and gun turrets.

The bombing started at approximately 12.57. The first Tallboy dropped, undershot by about 100 yards and caused so much debris and smoke that the other aircraft had to break off bombing runs, to come in for another or approach from a different heading. The first drop was probably from Flying Officer Leavitt's aircraft (DV380 'P'), a second bomb, dropped by Flying Officer Martin (DV393 'R') also undershot by about 100 yards, while Castagnola (LM492 'W') let his bomb got into a motor vessel, later identified as the minesweeper *M1*, in Eidsvag Bay, scoring a direct hit on its stern. It began to settle in the water immediately and about three minutes later either the boiler or ammunition on the ship, blew up and the ship rolled over and sank. Three of the crew were killed, seventeen listed as missing, four badly wounded and ten slightly wounded.

Flying Officer Watts also attacked a ship, the German tramp steamer *Olga Sierus* of 3,334 tons. His bomb was recorded as a near miss, but it caused a leak to such an extent that it had to be run aground at Sandvikena to avoid sinking. The force attacking the pens, under the control of Squadron Leader Brookes, came in, Brookes dropping his bomb at 12.58 into the south-west corner of the pens. Flight Lieutenant Goodman made four or five runs. They could have dropped on their first but the bomb sight became u/s. The others had mixed fortunes, some having to bring their bombs home when the target became too obscured to bomb with any

135

accuracy and to avoid hitting civilian-occupied areas. However, the others put three bombs onto the pens, the bombs getting through the 2½-3½ metre thick concrete roof. Damage was also done to workshops, offices and storerooms. *U-775* remained undamaged by the blast, and *U-864* was only slightly damaged by falling chunks of concrete. Kapitän Rosing, commander of the U-Boat force in Norway, later reported severe damage at Lagosvag Harbour, with one submarine sunk, another damaged. *U-864* was later reported torpedoed off Bergen on 9th February with the total loss of its crew.

During the attack, casualties on the ground were light. Most of the Norwegians had taken to the shelters but two men of the Todt Organisation were killed near the pens and about a dozen Germans were injured. Three Norwegians were brought in from Lakosvag wounded. One severely injured man had not been able to reach a shelter in time and had the wall of a house fall on him. In all about ten civilians were injured but none killed. The raid ended at 1.56 p.m., the 'All Clear' sounded at 2.14.

The fighter force from Herdla, was 9/JG5, led by Oberleutnant Werner Gayko, and 12/JG5, led by Leutnant Rudolf Linz. Rudi Linz' victory total was nearing seventy, but he was destined to die in action on 9th February and receive a posthumous Knight's Cross in March 1945. These two *Staffel*, flying FW190s, came up to meet the Lancasters, the *Gruppe* having moved to Herdla from Bardufoss in mid-December to take part in the defence of western Norway. They followed the Lancasters for fifty miles on their homeward route but combats between the bombers and the fighters commenced around 1 o'clock over the target area.

Squadron Leader Tony Iveson had to change aircraft before take-off owing to engine trouble. The aircraft he took (NG 181) was hit over the target area by flak, and then attacked by a Focke Wulf from the starboard quarter. Its presence was reported to Iveson the very moment the tail fin on the port side was blasted away, and black smoke began to stream from the port inner engine. A second 190 came into attack, but was fired on by Pilot Officer Wass, just after he had heard a message from Iveson regarding the abandoning of the aircraft. Looking back into the Lancaster from his turret, he saw two members of the crew at the side exit –

Sergeant Smith and Flying Officer Alan Tippell. He decided to join them as the aircraft seemed doomed. All three baled out and Wass landed in soft snow up to his knees. He found he had landed on the side of a mountain but was soon picked up by the Germans and taken to Oslo. He was given a meal and a bed for the night and the next day taken to a nearby airfield which today is Oslo's main airport. Here he met Alan Tippell and also a member of John Pryor's crew who had also been shot down. Tippell had been shot at after landing on a German barracks. Wass ended up in Stalag Luft 13D until liberated by the Americans in May 1945.

Although he had little control over his crippled Lancaster, Iveson ordered his flight engineer to tie the control column in such a way as to ease the strain he was having to exert in trying to maintain level flight. In this way he managed to fly home and make a successful landing at Sumburgh, in the Shetlands. Flying Officer Watts also put his Lancaster down in the Shetlands, at Miltown. Tony Iveson was recommended for an immediate DFC.

Squadron Leader Brookes was also attacked by a FW190 over the target area, his rear gunner, Flight Lieutenant Arthur 'Jock' Farthing, returned its fire forcing the 190 to break off. He then told Brookes to corkscrew. His actions undoubtedly saved the aircraft from severe damage and he was later awarded the DFC.

Flying Officer James Castagnola was attacked three times by FW190s, but by skilful evasion tactics his aircraft was not hit. Another Lancaster was flying just below him on three engines, its port outer engine completely missing. It had been hit by flak over Bergen which severed the engine bearings, allowing the engine to drop right out of its mounting. Castagnola reduced height in order for his front gunner to help cover the cripple which was also being attacked by a Focke Wulf.

Flight Lieutenant John Pryor, aged twenty-six, was attacked repeatedly by two German fighters for thirty-seven minutes. He had already completed forty-five ops with 207 and 617 Squadrons, so was an experienced bomber captain. He lost height fast in a dive of 3,000 to 4,000 feet and they released their bomb in the dive. His two port engines were hit and Albert Hepworth, the rear gunner, had to turn his turret by hand. Hepworth was also on his 45th trip and felt sure it was to be his last. All the crew were given

137

the order to bale out at a height of about 15,000 feet, Pryor holding the aircraft steady while they all got out. They all landed on an island about forty miles north-west of Bergen. Sadly Flying Officer Kendrick's parachute failed to open properly and he was badly injured when hitting the ground. He was taken to the local schoolhouse and tended by the schoolteacher there. The Germans came to claim him, but were told he was too ill to be moved. He never gained consciousness and died shortly afterwards.

John Pryor had been performing wonders by flying the Lanc with two engines over and around the mountains surrounding Bergen. He made for sea level, all the while being hammered by the two 190s. He pulled the port wing over to the left when only a yard off the sea. The wireless operator had clamped his key down, and then made for the escape hatch. One fighter came up alongside the Lanc, the German pilot pointing upwards, as if to say, make height and bale out. They then fired a red distress flare to let the fighter know they were helpless.

Pryor pulled the bomber up to about 4,000 feet and baled out himself, his parachute only just opening in time before he crashed down into the snow. It was so soft he went down to a depth of about eight feet and had to pull himself out of the hole using the parachute lines. In doing so he suffered a rupture. Meanwhile the aeroplane crashed into the sea outside Fedje.

One of the 190s that had attacked them was shot down in the exchange and crashed. Its pilot, Ludwig Kircher, aged twenty, was killed. Another FW190 shot down in the air battle was flown by 21-year-old George Liber, who later died in hospital.

The survivors of Pryor's crew were rounded up and taken to Oslo where they met those of Iveson's crew who had baled out. They were then taken to Germany by sea. On arrival they were taken to an Oberlag interrogation centre near Frankfurt where they were interviewed by a German Fleet Air Arm officer. He seemed very well informed, and when he talked to Albert Hepworth, knew that he was a member of 617 Squadron, that the AOC of 5 Group was Cochrane, and he also knew every squadron commander and flight commander's aircraft letter and their station. He knew, too, that he and Pryor had both been in 207 Squadron earlier. He had photographs of Mess parties at the Petwood Hotel, orders of battle for 617 Squadron, and many other things that made them wonder if airfield security was all it should have been.

Another Lancaster attacked by 190s was that flown by Flying Officer Ian Ross, RAAF. Other Lancaster crews saw Ross' machine leaving a trail of smoke from one engine, and Flying Officer Watts asked permission of the force leader to leave the target area to assist them. Permission was given but by this time Ross was low over the sea with fighters snapping after him. Freddie Watts went into a dive from about 3,000 feet with a speed building up to 350 mph, his front gunner blazing away at the enemy fighters. The 190s retreated and Ross was able to make a perfect ditching on the sea.

Shortly afterwards the crew were seen on the fuselage. Watts by this time was putting out an SOS distress call on the radio, and then stayed in the area, circling the ditched aircraft and crew for about fifty minutes. He finally had to leave them as his fuel began to run low. Castagnola had also gone to the assistance of Ross and had also remained over the downed crew, even dropping Mae Wests and anything else that might help the men in the water. Castagnola's wireless operator, Bill Eaves, managed to get a message to the air-sea-rescue aircraft.

Before the Warwick aircraft arrived, a Beaufighter of No 18 Group sighted the ditched aircraft's dinghy and also sent a distress signal. The Warwick arrived about 5.45 p.m. and an airborne lifeboat was dropped which landed in the sea about 200 yards from the dinghy. One of the crew was seen to climb aboard the lifeboat and then the rest of the crew were seen making their way towards it. One half of the Lancaster was still afloat and oil was seen on the sea.

The Warwick aircraft had then to leave the area quickly due to the arrival of an enemy aircraft, thought to be a Junkers 88, which proceeded to strafe the men and the lifeboat. The German pilot could hardly miss, the sea was calm and the visibility good.

A Catalina later made a thorough search of the whole area, right up to the Norwegian coast, even using a Leigh Light, but nothing was seen or found of the boat or crew, not by it nor by searching aircraft which flew out the next day. Only the body of the wireless operator, Flying Officer Mawbray Ellwood, aged twenty-four, was given up by the sea. It was washed up on the Isle of Asner in the Arctic Circle on the 13th.

Ian Ross and his crew were a great loss to the squadron. They had taken part in many operations with 617, including the attacks on *Tirpitz*. For them to die in such a way after surviving the ditching seems particularly tragic. Once again fate had taken its toll.

The crews of 9 Squadron, had not been briefed with the same instructions as 617. Whereas 617 were to fly in low over the water, do a 90° turn to the right and fly down the fjord to Bergen, 9 Squadron flew in at full height, flying over the land to reach Bergen.

They too ran into enemy fighters and several running battles were had with the 190s. Flying Officer Harper was attacked by two, Flight Lieutenant March by five and Flight Lieutenant Ray Harris' rear gunner reported four Mustangs behind, which turned out to be 190s. They attacked the Lancaster and the rear man, Bill Gabriel, was hit in the legs. The attacks lasted for seventeen minutes and Harris threw his aircraft all over the sky in an attempt to shake them off. At the end of the attack he was completely defenceless. All his turrets had been put out of action and to make matters worse one of the 190s came alongside on his port wing and he could see the pilot smiling at him. This enraged Ray so much that he took out his revolver and fired at the 190 through his side window. He didn't hit it but it made him feel a whole lot better. With great skill he managed to fly home to land at Carnaby in Yorkshire. Gabriel was later awarded the DFC, Harris having been awarded a DFC a few weeks earlier. Flight Lieutenant Price returned without being able to bomb, with several flak holes in his Lancaster.

After the raid, the Germans reported two British aircraft shot down by Luftwaffe fighters and two FW190s lost to enemy action. The German propaganda machine then reported nine British aircraft shot down by fighters and flak. A later report claimed thirteen shot down, nine to fighters, two by flak; the reason for the other two of the thirteen was not given. In yet another report in a Bergen newspaper the total RAF losses rose to twenty-five! This report made no mention of a ship being sunk and other damage,

140

but did go on to say that many of the attacking aircraft were damaged and that many of them would have been unable to reach England.

The Lancaster crews in turn claimed five FW190s damaged, and a Mosquito claimed a 190 damaged. The fighter escort reported seeing nothing of the German aircraft over the target and one can only assume they were flying at a different height than the bombers. A report said it was difficult to escort bombers who bombed a target from different directions. The opinion of the bomber crews, however, was that the ever aggressive Polish pilots had gone down to a lower level, attacking targets on the ground, and had not paid enough attention to what was happening above them. It does seem a little strange that they did not see any German fighters, when one recalls the number of combats taking place. An enquiry was set up afterwards to determine why the Mustang pilots failed to intercept the Germans. It was stated in this enquiry that the bombers had split up and bombed from all heights and angles.

The German fighters had probably come up from below to make their attacks when the Mustangs were at the opposite side of the target area, which was some twenty miles in diameter. On the 13th, six Mustangs of 315 Squadron and six Spitfires of 441 Squadron were part of the search mission to find the crew of Ross' Lancaster.

The squadron's post mortem findings on this operation were that insufficient time was allowed for the climb to bombing height and this made formation even worse.

Between December 1944 and March 1945, the weather caused difficulties for flying, and for the crews. The rear gunner, particularly, had little to protect him from the bitter cold during this time of year. Only his perspex turret was between him and temperatures down to anything as much as 40° below, and most rear gunners had the centre perspex area taken out to improve visibility. The amount of clothing worn and the care taken putting on this clothing and all the equipment were most important. No experienced air gunner would remove his gloves to clear a blockage of his guns; to do so would invite severe frost bite to the extent of losing his fingers. The other problem was the electrically-heated flying suit which could cause blisters on the feet due to excessive sweating. Another, and very important, problem was keeping the oxygen pipe clear of ice. To do this one had periodically to keep pinching the tube. To touch any metal in the aircraft without gloves on would result in skin being left on it.

On one occasion during these three months when there was no flying, a horse was brought in to a sergeants mess dance, by two members of 617. Sergeant Matthews, of Freddie Watts' crew, climbed onto its back and rode it round the Mess with the band playing and everybody clapping and cheering. When the farmer who owned the animal found out, he was amazed as he had never had the courage to go near the animal, let alone ride it!

At about this time, the longest serving member of 617 Squadron was posted to RAF Padgate on a compassionate posting. Flight Sergeant George Powell, known to everyone as 'Chiefy', had joined the RAF in 1928 and became an air gunner with 2 Squadron. In 1939 when war began, he was with 500 Squadron at Manston, flying in Ansons which he described in 1982 as 'the flying bullet'. Later in the war he went to 57 Squadron at Scampton, where 617 was later formed. When 617 came into being in early 1943, he and Sergeant Jim Heveron had licked the ground crews into shape in about two days. During his time with 617 he saw all the commanding officers through their initial periods with the squadron and in these two years many members of both air and ground crews had cause to be grateful to George for his help and guidance. In his own words, 'The squadron during this time, was my life. I many a time gave up the chance of leave to stay with the squadron.'

It was not until February that the weather allowed further operations to be flown, the first coming on the 3rd. The target on this date was midget submarine pens at Poortershaven, Holland. Eighteen Lancasters, escorted by two squadrons of Spitfires, headed out, led by Johnnie Fauquier.

During the attack, direct hits were recorded by Squadron Leader Brookes and Squadron Leader Powell, but it was difficult to assess all the bomb hits because of smoke. Three or four bombs were seen to fall into the water and one landed in a field. Flight Lieutenant Gavin had a 30-40 yard overshoot while Castagnola's overshoot

142

was 50-75 yards, although it fell on a railway line to the north of the target.

Four large buildings east of the basin were destroyed or severely damaged and 160 feet of wharf was knocked out of alignment. The electric rail line between Maashus and Van Holland appeared to be cut by three large craters and a large building was destroyed by two direct hits and at least one near miss. One third of the roof of another building was missing and yet another was smashed by a near miss, with a fourth damaged.

Six Lancasters were hit by flak, those flown by Fauquier, Calder, Flatman, Castagnola, Gumbley and Sanders, but with Fauquier's leadership, the attack had been very accurate and highly concentrated. This raid was mentioned in Farquier's citation when he received a second bar to his DSO.

Three days later 617 went back to Germany to bomb the Bielefeld railway viaducts over the River Werre, standing on the main line from Berlin to the Ruhr and situated $2\frac{1}{2}$ miles northeast of the centre of Bielefeld. The viaducts were 27 feet wide at track level, each carrying a double track supported by a gap of about seven feet at track level. Each viaduct consisted of 26 arches each with a span of about 46 feet, a height of $72\frac{1}{2}$ feet, and the overall length was 384 yards. It had been attacked on a number of occasions since November 1944 by the American 8th Air Force carrying 500 and 1,000-lb bombs but was still in operation. 617 detailed seventeen aircraft but weather again was the main enemy and the operation was aborted, with four Lancasters being damaged by flak for their pains.

Two days later, on the 8th, the target was once again the U-Boat pens at Ijmuiden. Fifteen Lancasters lifted off into the wintry sky, but the weather was better with only small amounts of cloud around. Rendezvous was made with three RAF Spitfire squadrons from 11 Group as they headed out over the sea.

The Lancasters went in at 15,000 feet, Fauquier leading. He saw two direct hits, and Calder and Castagnola also observed hits and a near miss. Flying Officer Martin saw three near misses, while Brookes saw his bomb fall on the entrance of the northern half of the target. Flight Lieutenant Price saw two near misses. On the northern end of the pens, the roof was destroyed and the harbour

143

wall damaged, and despite heavy flak only four aircraft were damaged – Calder's, Sanders', Gumbley's and Flight Lieutenant Lancey's.

During this period, living at the Petwood Hotel had its amusing moments. In the grounds of the hotel was a tin hut which served as a cinema and was known to the crews as the 'flicks'. In the gardens of the hotel was a pond and on dark nights it was the custom to invite new arrivals to visit the flicks. Two or more established members of the squadron would walk on either side of the newcomer and guide him towards the pond. At the last moment, they would peel off and leave the unfortunate sprog to a dip.

The Dagenham Girl Pipers paid a visit to Woodhall Spa and were later invited over to the Petwood, the air around echoing to the sounds of the pipes.

On St Valentine's Day, 617 tried for the Bielefeld viaducts once again, but cloud again thwarted the nineteen aircraft detailed, and they had to abort.

There was a change of establishment a week later when it was decided to expand 617 from two flights to three. One would retain the Tallboy bomb-carrying Lancasters; the others would equip with Lancasters able to carry a new bomb – the 22,000 lb (ten ton) 'Grand Slam' bomb. This almost doubled 617's hitting power and again confirmed them as the most destructive unit in the RAF.

As this was happening, the third attempt to hit the Bielefeld Viaducts was made. This time the weather did not oppose them and Fauquier led a force of eighteen aircraft into the attack. Flying Officer W.A. Daniels, Fauquier's bomb aimer, dropped his bomb on their second run from 13,660 feet and it was seen to overshoot by about fifty yards. Flying Officer D.W. Carey also had an overshoot as did Flight Lieutenant Price on his third run. Squadron Leader Calder claimed a direct hit with his Tallboy and quite a few near misses were seen. In fact two pieces of the viaduct were destroyed by near misses. One near miss caused 95 feet of the northern viaduct to collapse and subsidence caused from a direct hit, for a distance of 135 feet under two tracks.

The next operation, against Ladbergen, on the 24th was called off due to weather and 10/10th cloud.

Three new crews arrived during February, those of Squadron Leader Gordon, and Flight Lieutenants Rawes and Trent. Shortly after his arrival, Gordon was ordered to collect one of the newly modified Lancasters that could carry the Grand Slam. After a check out, all the aircraft would be collected from Coningsby and flown to Woodhall. When Gordon went to pick this one up it was late in the day and he couldn't find a crew to go with him so he decided to go alone. The ground crew at Coningsby were a little surprised to discover Gordon alone, but nevertheless allowed him to take the Lancaster. The 617 ground crew at Woodhall, however, were not at all happy when they found out that they had missed a golden opportunity of a free ride in their favourite type of aeroplane, and a new one at that. If asked, they would have gladly gone with him.

There was a new AOC at 5 Group now, Air Vice-Marshal Constantine. He had seen the photographs of the Bielefeld Viaduct raid and sent a message of congratulations to 617 and added, 'Keep up the training, we can't afford to put these new little pets in the wrong place.' He meant, of course, the new Grand Slam bombs.

CHAPTER FIFTEEN

Grand Slam

The squadron was given a respite before their next operation, which did not take place until 9th March. Yet again the target was the Bielefeld viaduct. They were able to navigate to it without the aid of maps, having been so many times recently, but once again it was aborted because of weather.

Four days later the mission was attempted again, and again it was scrubbed out. Group Captain Fauquier and Squadron Leader Calder were carrying Grand Slams for the first time and the Lancasters carried new markings of 'YZ' rather than the old 'AJ'. The aircraft still came under fire from the ground, and four Lancasters had been hit, including Calder's 'S'. The Met boys were not very popular with Fauquier and Calder, who had been forced to return with their Grand Slams aboard. They had had to use the whole length of the runway to get their heavily loaded Lancasters airborne, and so Fauquier decided they should use the base at Carnaby for a landing which had a longer runway than Woodhall. This was accomplished without incident, although Calder's crew said with feeling that it was the best landing Jock had ever achieved since joining 617! The two pilots had, of course, created history in being the first men to land with a ten-ton bomb on board.

The bomb was very powerful as demonstrated on 13th March, when a test drop at Ashley Walk Bombing Range, produced a crater 30 feet deep and 124 feet in diameter.

They returned to the viaduct the next day, and once again Fauquier and Calder were to carry the big bombs. It had been felt that the type of concrete structure which the Germans used, would need a larger and deeper penetration bomb, and the minimum weight of bomb which would cause satisfactory damage to such targets was 22,000 pounds. Its case was a casting of special chrome of Molyodenium Steel with a total weight of Torpex D/I of some 9,500 pounds. With this bomb it was not so important to obtain a direct hit, for the 'earthquake' effect from a near miss would surely cause any such structure as a viaduct, to just crumble away.

On take-off from Carnaby, Squadron Leader Calder saw that Fauquier's aircraft was still at dispersal with one engine stopped. A connecting rod had broken, and his bomb sight had gone u/s due to an oil leak. On this occasion the sight was the most important part of the aircraft. Fauquier signalled to Jock Calder that he would fly his aircraft, but Calder, however, declined to understand the signal, rather like Nelson at Trafalgar 140 years earlier, and proceeded to take off. With this Fauquier started to run down the runway trying to stop him, but to no avail. It was only after they were airborne that Calder began to realise the position he was in. It was now up to him and his crew to plant the biggest bomb of the war in the right place, or face an even more angry CO on their return. His historic take-off time was recorded at 1.46 p.m.

To carry this huge bomb needed a specially designed Lancaster with a cut-away bomb bay and strengthened undercarriage, and also the fitting of four 1,280 hp Rolls Royce Merlin engines. This aircraft was known as the B1 Special. To lessen the take-off weight no wireless operator or mid-upper gunner was carried.

Fourteen other aircraft of 617 flew out on the 14th, all carrying normal Tallboy bombs, and the force was escorted by eight squadrons of Mustangs plus four Oboe-marking Mosquitos of 8 PFF Group. There was no cloud below 13,000 feet but considerable haze. On the way to the viaduct a squadron of Flying Fortresses were seen leaving the Bielefeld area having bombed nearby installations.

To make things worse for Calder and his crew on arrival at the target, cloud covered the northern end of the viaduct preventing a bomb run from north to south. Calder skirted the target to make an approach from the south. Flight Lieutenant John Benison, gave Crafer, the bomb aimer, amended settings for the SABS in double-quick time. Then they settled down for the run in. Crafer switched on the bomb sight to start a straight and level approach, gave Calder one or two minor corrections and then released the bomb at

4.28 p.m., from a height of 11,965 feet..

Immediately the Lancaster rose up, Crafer being shot up from the floor to come down again with a thud which knocked the breath out of him. So great was the sudden loss of weight, the aircraft had risen some 500 feet in height. Calder could do nothing about this but he quickly regained his senses and turning, picked out the bomb as it fell towards the target. Because of an 11-second fuse he did not see the actual explosion, but suddenly, over the intercom came a yell, 'You've done it!' It was the pilot of the Mosquito photographic aircraft, Warrant Officer Player, DFC of 627 Squadron. His cameraman, Pilot Officer Heath, filmed the whole attack from 4.15 to 4.35 p.m. With this, Calder swung the aircraft round to have a look for himself and saw that at least 100 yards of the viaduct had collapsed.

Johnnie Fauquier never really forgave Jock Calder or his crew, but he was big enough not to take any action and in fact put Calder up for a bar to his DSO.

In fact some 200 feet of the north viaduct and 260 feet of the southern viaduct were destroyed as well as three main spars. Photographs showed the viaduct had been wrecked and a direct hit by a Tallboy on the south-west approaches, had completely blocked all lines.

Flight Lieutenant Rawes dropped the Tallboy on a crossroads 750 yards from the target by mistake; Flying Officer Carey brought his bomb back when his sight went u/s, and Sayers lost his bomb when the bomb doors opened and it just fell out.

By now 617 Squadron was used to making history, and on this day they made history yet again.

The next day, just two 617 aircraft took off, each carrying Grand Slams. The pilots were Calder and Cockshott, and they flew in company with fourteen aircraft of 9 Squadron. Their target was another viaduct, the Arnsberg railway viaduct, another important supply line of the Germans. It consisted of five spars 425 feet long, 35-40 feet high and spanned the River Ruhr at Arnsberg. It was built of brick and masonry, faced with cement, and it carried two tracks. The US 8th Air Force had attacked it twice with 1,000-lb bombs and 9 Squadron had twice tried on 13th and 14th March, with Tallboys. No direct hits were recorded; most of the bombs fell on the east side and only minor damage was caused.

Squadron Leader J.V. Cockshott dropped his Grand Slam at 4.56 p.m. from 13,000 feet on his fourth run. Calder brought his back, as he could not see the target for cloud, landing at Manston. When asked by Manston's Duty Officer what bomb-load he had, Calder answered, '22,000 pounds.' The DO was shocked, having never seen or probably heard of such a bomb-load.

Cockshott, a Yorkshireman from Bradford, was on his 57th trip and he later compared this operation with his first daylight trip to Milan, when he had a bomb-load of a mere 4,000 lbs in March 1943. He said afterwards, 'It's really worthwhile to carry one of these. The bomb aiming is perfect; down goes the bomb and up goes your aircraft.' The viaduct, however, survived.

Flying Officer Daniels, DFC, a Canadian from Manitoba, who had flown as bomb aimer to both Cheshire and Tait, said, 'I wish we had had this bomb in time for the *Tirpitz* operations.' Memories from the men who carried the Grand Slam bomb recall the distinct 'Bomp' after the bomb struck. The aircraft modified to carry them was known by the crews as a 'Clapper' for after dropping the bomb, one would go like the clappers!

With the failure of the 15th still fresh in their minds, the squadron was detailed back to Arnsberg on 19th March. During the briefing, the crews were warned that a hospital stood near the target and must be avoided at all costs. Farquier led 617 and on approaching the target saw there was a large water dam on the port side. The Germans thought that this might be the target and set up a smoke screen, but to no avail as 617 sailed on past towards the viaduct. The hospital was clearly visible and not hit in the attack, much to the relief of the crews.

No 463 Squadron filmed the Grand Slams leaving the aircraft and recorded one striking the western end of the viaduct. Two spans were completely cut while railway tracks were extensively damaged. The pilot who dropped it was Flying Officer Phil Martin (PG996 'C'). This magnificent historical film can now be seen at the Imperial War Museum.

Flying Officer Spiers saw his bomb hit the side of the bridge, while Fauquier's undershot slightly. Flight Lieutenant Gumbley's Grand Slam (or Special Store as it was also called in 617's operations book) hit 50 yards short of the aiming point. Flight Lieutenant Sayers made two runs but could not get his bomb to release. Flight Lieutenant Dobson recorded a direct hit and Flight Lieutenant Gavin's bomb fell into the smoke of about five previous bombs. Flatman recorded his Grand Slam as falling about 30 yards from the viaduct.

An intact part of a Grand Slam was found at Arnsberg at the end of the war still with most of its explosive filling. It seemed probable the bomb became unstable and made a flat landing on a road. The rear powder then detonated, leaving the filling in the forward end of the bomb still intact. The front part of a Tallboy was also found intact at Arnsberg; its point of impact was a masonry wall immediately above the resting place of the empty case. The structure of the wall did not permit the nose of the bomb to get sufficient bite to penetrate and explode.

Two spans of the viaduct, measuring 100 feet, collapsed into the river while the embankment was cut for over a distance of 115 feet, by a bomb which fell at its base 300 yards west of the river.

The weather was clear on the 21st and twenty aircraft took off for Bremen to attack the Arbergen railway bridge over the River Weser, near Nienburg. Two aircraft carried Grand Slams, one flown by Calder, one by Fauquier, Calder dropped his from 13,000 feet on a railway line just thirty yards short of the bridge while Fauquier's fell 200 yards north of the bridge. The remainder of the aircraft, carrying Tallboys, bombed successfully. Cockshott's bomb fell very near to the first stanchion of the bridge. Flight Lieutenant Gavin's bomb was presumed to have gone wide as his bomb sight went u/s just after making his bomb run. He finally dropped his bomb manually after following another aircraft on its run. He was then hit by flak and his port outer engine caught fire as he turned away. Flying Officer Len Burrows, an Australian, saw two direct hits on the bridge and also saw a jet-propelled fighter coming down out of the sun! There was just enough time to warn his pilot and open fire, before feeling the German's cannon shells ripping through the Lancaster. It did not do major damage and the fire in the engine was put out, enabling Gavin to reach base safely.

Flight Lieutenant Bernard 'Barney' Gumbley, aged twenty-nine, from New Zealand, was not so lucky. This was his 18th trip with 617 following a successful tour with 49 Squadron. His Lancaster was hit by flak in the target area and went down. A farmer and the *Bürgermeister* of Okel, saw Gumbley's aircraft crash at about 11 o'clock, about 300 metres from Hauslengshaus, one kilometre from Okel. The *Bürgermeister* described the explosion as unbelievable; the crater it caused was ten metres deep. Gumbley and his crew were all killed instantly.

The large, single, overhanging span of the bridge was broken at the centre and fell sagging into the river. The spars at each end were torn from their supporting pier. The one on the east side of the river fell to the ground, and the one on the west was badly twisted and sagging on the ground at one end. Part of the elevated track between the end of the embankment and the first pier on the west side of the river was destroyed.

At de-briefing it was felt that more support was needed for attacks against heavily defended targets. During the raid five aircraft were hit by flak, those flown by Fauquier, which was hit six times, Gavin, Price, Spiers and Dobson.

The next day, twenty aircraft took off to take out the Nienburg railway bridge. Conditions were ideal, with no cloud and good visibility. Fourteen aircraft carried Tallboys, with one-hour delayed fuses and six with Grand Slams with 25-30 second fuses.

Squadron Leader Gordon saw his bomb fall as a near miss and reported the bridge as collapsed at the end of the attack. Squadron Leader Cockshott reported a direct hit, but Squadron Leader Powell ran into trouble. Unable to release their bomb on the first or second runs, by the time he was ready for a third run the bridge had been destroyed, so he had to bring it back. Flight Lieutenant Rawes believed his bomb to have gone through the eastern end of the bridge.

All the spars were broken or torn off the bridge, and the target was struck off Bomber Command's list when a photo recce aircraft brought back pictures of the smashed bridge.

On the 23rd, a whole hangar at Woodhall Spa was devoted to fitting new undercarriages to the Lancasters that carried the Grand

Slams. These undercarriages were those designed for the new Avro Lincoln aircraft, which were just about to be brought into service. They had a pressure of 800 PSI instead of the usual 400 PSI, which was necessary to take the weight of the 22,000 pounders.

An operation was flown on the same day, against another bridge, this time the railway bridge at Bremen. Twenty Lancasters took off, fourteen carrying Tallboys and six Grand Slams. The weather was ideal for precision bombing but to get to the target they had to run the gauntlet of Bremen's tough defences.

Flight Lieutenant Lancey (NG489 'M') was hit by flak over the centre of Bremen which made his bombsight u/s; Grant Perry, the bomb aimer, had to jettison their bomb immediately, to enable Lancey to regain control of the badly damaged Lancaster. On return to base, the aircraft was found to be only good for spare parts!

Flight Lieutenant E.V. Gavin (PD134 'Y') was attacked by a Messerschmitt 262 jet fighter and lost his starboard outer engine; he also found the flak very intense. Squadron Leader Brookes' machine was hit by flak in the target area but reported seeing three direct hits on the bridge and two near misses just south of it. One of these was scored by Fauquier, who was leading the squadron. His bomber was also hit by flak as was Jock Calder's, who had his clear vision panel shattered. Three aircraft returned with faults, two with engine problems and Trent with a total oxygen failure. His crew were a little worried about having to land carrying a Grand Slam, but Trent was a good pilot and managed it with little trouble.

Gavin was not the only pilot to be attacked by Me262s, on the Bremen raid. A total of fifteen were seen en route to the target, and four Lancasters were attacked though luckily without a single loss. On the return trip, Fauquier saw a badly damaged Flying Fortress limping back to England on two engines. It was alone and flying at 4,000 feet. He ordered the squadron to carry on to base, while he went down and escorted the American bomber back across the sea.

Another event that occurred on the 23rd was the arrival of a Lancaster model as used on the Dams Raid. It had been in storage since mid-1943. It was needed now in order to carry old 'Upkeep' mines (as used on the Dams Raid) out to sea to be jettisoned, without their fuses of course.

The operation for the 27th was an attack against construction works connected with U-Boats at Farge, five miles north of Vegesack, Bremen. Hitler had ordered the construction and building of the works in 1942. Shortly after work began, a decision was reached by Albert Speer's Ministry's Main Committee, for ship building, to resort to the building of individual sections, and the assembly of prefabricated Submarines, Type XXI. 'Valentin' – the code word for Vegesack, was selected for the assembly plant. The intention was to assemble fourteen submarines each month and by August 1945 be·in a position to stop production in vulnerable open air assembly yards of the Blöhm und Voss works in Hamburg and Deschimag, in Bremen. The planned submarine production was three in March, six in April, nine in May, twelve in June and July and then fourteen in August.

The length of the assembly plant was 1,370 feet by 315 feet wide. Its height was 96 feet above ground, 41 below ground. the roof was composed of reinforced concrete, arched trusses placed close together on the walls. The space between and above them being filled with concrete.

For this operation twenty Lancasters were scheduled, escorted by eight Mustang squadrons from 11 Group. Flak was slight, enemy fighters non-existent, while the visibility over the target was good. Thirteen of the aircraft carried Grand Slams and seven Tallboys, each bomb being set with one-hour fuses.

Flight Lieutenant Goodman had to abandon the show just after take-off, and Lancey had to abort over the target when his port inner engine failed. It was his first op with a Grand Slam and could not keep up with the others, so he was ordered to drop it into the North Sea. He never again had the opportunity of carrying a Grand Slam on operations.

Flight Lieutenant Trent's aircraft was hit by flak on its bombing run but carried on and bombed. Flying Officer Richardson, on Trent's crew, recalls, 'The jolt from the bomb leaving the was much more severe than the worst flak I could ever remember.' The Flight Lieutenant's Lancaster was hit eight times and his navigator, Flight Lieutenant Gorringe, slightly wounded.

Of the seventeen aircraft that managed to bomb, fourteen hits were recorded, two of which were Grand Slams which hit the roof almost in the centre of the building and penetrated five to six feet before detonating. The explosions brought down a considerable mass of concrete, weighing approximately 800 tons per crater. Flying Officer Len Sumpter, DFC, DFM, of Marshall's crew, was on his 50th operation, and said of it, 'The weather was perfect for the raid. The fairly heavy flak was accurate but did not deter the raiders from achieving a very good concentration on the aiming point. I saw four direct hits that seemed to penetrate the roof of the plant. From our height, they seemed like little puffs of dust; when those puffs cleared you could see the black holes they had left behind.' Sumpter had flown with 617 on the famous Dams Raid, and had returned for a second tour with the squadron in January 1945. Another original Dambuster in Marshall's crew was Dougie Webb, DFM.

During the month of March 1945, 156 day operational sorties were despatched – 156 aircraft – flying 717 hours on ops. On these sorties, thirty-one Grand Slams and forty Tallboys were dropped. During the period December to March, the bombing accuracy of 617 and 9 Squadrons, while carrying Tallboys, was analysed. Although they used different bomb sights, and bombing heights varied between 9,000 and 17,000 feet, it was found that 617 had the greater accuracy. Of the plotted bombs, only 1% of 617's bombs were gross errors; 9 Squadron recorded 10%. A gross error was any bomb falling more than 400 yards from the aiming point.

The target for 6th April was an old one for 617 – the port at Ijmuiden. Specifically the target was a blockade runner or *Sperrbrecher*, reported to be in the harbour. Jock Calder led a force of fourteen Lancasters, all carrying Tallboys, and they were escorted by Spitfires of 602 and 603 Squadrons.

Calder, Gordon and Price all dropped their bombs at 9.43 a.m. from 14,500 feet, but the weather was proving hopeless, and Calder had to abandon the raid. As in the past, it was a case of 'if not today, then tomorrow', but the job had to be done. So on the 7th, 617 returned for another try.

154

The force was exactly the same, but it was Squadron Leader Cockshott who was in the lead plane. The Lancasters sailed in over the target, let go their bombs and as they flew off the ship appeared to be settling down at the stern, with the afterdecks awash – the vessel was probably sitting on the bottom. Flying Officer Leavitt, who hailed from America, claimed a direct hit on his second run, the bomb having failed to release on the first.

The 9th brought another U-boat target, this time the pens at Hamburg. With an escort of Spitfires and Mustangs, seventeen Lancasters flew there, two carrying Grand Slams. Flak over the target was as heavy as expected, and the aircraft of Calder, Powell, McLoughlin, Leavitt, Warburton and Marshall were all hit. There was also quite a bit of fighter activity, including German jet fighters. Crews who took part still remember today the sight of the fighters of both sides, dropping the wing tanks as the battle developed. Nearby other squadrons were bombing the oil refineries in Hamburg with 1,000-pounders.

Five direct hits were claimed and plot photographs confirmed seven hits, four of which penetrated the roof. Most of the buildings west and north of the pens were destroyed or severely damaged.

The operation on 13th April was the first of three attacks on the German pocket battleship *Lützow* and the heavy-cruiser *Prinz Eugen* in the Baltic. Based in the Baltic Ocean at Swinemünde, they were used for shore bombardment, supply and evacuation duties. Twenty Lancasters flew out, each carrying twelve 1,000 lb bombs, but the attacks were unsuccessful due to cloud. Flak was heavy, and Leavitt had two petrol tanks holed. One of his crew, Colin Cole, celebrated his 21st birthday on this date – it was also Sir Arthur Harris's 53rd birthday.

Trent's aircraft was hit by flak, damaging the windscreen. Flying Officer Richardson asked Trent how it had happened, Trent saying that he had spat on the windscreen and it broke!

The squadron sought out the big ships again on the 15th, but this time, of the twenty Lancasters, seventeen carried Tallboys and the other three 1,000-pounders. Yet again weather foiled any attempts to bomb, so it was back to the Baltic again on the 16th. This time eighteen aircraft went, fourteen with Tallboys. They were escorted by Mustangs of 442 and 611 Squadrons. Squadron Leader Brookes had gone sick and so one of his crew, Flying Officer Bird, flew with Squadron Leader Powell. As it turned out, this had tragic consequences.

The weather was excellent but a good deal of flak was encountered from the nearby town of Swinemünde. As they approached the ship, flying level for twenty minutes on the run in, the flak was intense and there were orange shell bursts all around them. Because the flak was so heavy they decided to fly in in full force instead of splitting up into sections to bomb. Flight Lieutenant Gavin was hit on the run and had to jettison his bomb over the target area. It overshot by about 450 yards. Johnnie Fauquier was also hit and so was Squadron Leader Gordon, his throttle controls being severed, causing the carburettor butterfly valve to close which lost him power in the port outer engine. This in turn spoilt his bombing run. His next run was not accurate so he decided to call it a day and was ordered to drop his bomb on a built-up area on the homeward route.

Flight Lieutenant Anning's machine was hit by flak but not before he put his bomb alongside the *Lützow*. In addition the Lancasters of Rawes, Hill, Flatman, Spiers, Castagnola and Quinton were hit and damaged. Squadron Leader John Powell's Lancaster (EG228 'V') was hit in the port engine in the first barrage. It caught fire and the bomber slowly rolled over and went down. Near the ground its port wing and part of the tail structure broke away. One parachute was seen to open at about 2,000 feet, shortly before the aircraft crashed at Caseburg, five miles south of Swinemünde. Powell and all his crew were killed. It would seem that he had something of a scratch crew, for Bird had come from Brookes' crew for this trip and Flight Lieutenant Mike Clarke was on his first trip of his second tour, having only joined 617 thirteen days earlier. Powell was just two weeks off his thirtieth birthday.

With the end of the war seemingly in sight, it seemed to some of the crews it had been a futile operation and the loss of a good crew. The ship, however, suffered direct hits and it was down by the stern after the attack. One Tallboy burst alongside it, the underwater explosion smashing the armour plating. On the *Lützow* at the time were six 11″ guns including a new model of gun from Krupps, which could fire projectiles with the weight of one ton and a range of 30,000 yards.

The ship took about two days to sink. Each day 617 were anxiously enquiring of the PRU if in fact it had gone down, for if it hadn't it would mean yet another try. Not a happy prospect considering the flak defences at Swinemünde. The *Prinz Eugen* was finally surrendered to the British at Copenhagen in May 1945, then despatched to America where it was later used in the Bikini Atom Bomb tests in 1946. It was finally sunk at Enubuj in December 1947.

In order to prevent the Germans from stopping Allied entry into the Elbe and Weser estuaries, the Heligoland guns needed to be destroyed. Bomber Command had been asked by SHAEF on 31st March as to how they might tackle the problem of neutralising the guns of Heligoland and how quickly they might be able to undertake the task. To have attempted to attack them with naval forces would have been plain suicide for they would have had to sail 20,000 yards under heavy coastal fire before they could even get within range to fire back. The agreed plan, then, was for the RAF to drop 1,000-lb bombs on the isle of Heligoland and the associate island of Bune.

First, however, the flak positions would need to be silenced, for there were at least forty heavy flak guns in the vicinity. After these flak points had been knocked out it would be possible to destroy the heavy guns with Tallboys and Grand Slams, but they could only be destroyed by direct hits or very near misses and each gun offered a very small target, not more than 60 feet in diameter. The plan was forwarded to Air Ministry by Bomber Command HQ on 4th April.

On 16th April the request for such an operation to be put into effect was sent to Bomber Command. It was a formidable task. Heligoland was made up of many sandbanks and the greater part was an airfield. It had two main coastal defence batteries, one of 12″ guns, the other of 6″ guns. There was also radar coverage of the western approaches to the Elbe and Weser estuaries. Two days later, Bomber Command sent 953 bombers to attack the batteries and they did in fact succeed in knocking out some of the guns and flak. To finish the job, however, Bomber Command sent 617 in with their big bombs.

The squadron was joined by those of 9 Squadron, and the force was escorted by six Spitfire and one Mustang squadron. Of 617 Squadron, thirteen carried Tallboys and six took Grand Slams. Bombing was reported accurate and several hits were seen. Photographs later showed the whole area saturated with bomb craters. The operation was filmed and this can be viewed at the Imperial War Museum.

The 25th April 1945 brought the last operation of the war for 617: the target was Hitler's mountain retreat, Berchtesgaden. Hitler had found this hideout in 1923 and he later built the Villa Berghof there. He also rented the Villa Wachenfeld in the same locality, which overlooked Berchtesgaden. Berghof was the only home which Hitler ever possessed.

The former British Prime Minister, Lloyd George, visited him there in 1936 and returned to Britain convinced Hitler was a great man. Only three years later Poland's fate and the start of the Second World War was decided there in August 1939.

The operation would encompass a round trip of 1,400 miles and the total force employed by Bomber Command was 350 aircraft. These were escorted by two Mustang fighter groups from the American 8th Air Force, totalling 98 aircraft. Of the force, 617 Squadron provided sixteen Lancasters, led by Squadron Leader Brookes, as Farquier, as he explained at the briefing, had been ordered to cease operational flying. He was visibly upset by the order, as his usual crisp uncompromising approach was badly lacking on this occasion. His words at the briefing were to the point:

'I'd like to have this target in my log book, Brookes; in fact I would like to have this target tatooed on my arse, but you have got to lead it.'

This kept up the tradition of the CO's of 617. Every one of them since May 1943 had to be ordered to stop flying after many sorties over and above what might normally be expected of them. Each battle order that was posted, always had the CO's name first, a wonderful example of a boss who knew he was leading a special bunch of guys.

For this historic operation, 617, followed by 9 Squadron, were to lead the whole force as a grand finale. They made rendezvous over Paris and approached Berchtesgaden from the southwest after flying along the line of the Alps. It seemed everybody wanted to bomb first. The flak was heavy and considerably accurate from hillside positions and from a nearby SS barracks. Flak from the 'Eagle's Nest' and Chalet was never more than slight, and inaccurate. The target was roughly 3,000-4,000 feet above sea level and was bombed in cloudless conditions, but with some local mist and snow on the mountains. Squadron Leader Brookes was unable to identify the target in time, nor did Squadron Leader Ward and Flight Lieutenant Gavin. Flight Lieutenant Goodman was hit by flak, but managed to drop his bomb. Leavitt did not bomb the target but dropped his bomb on a nearby viaduct over a road.

It was proving a difficult target to spot, but three crews bombed though did not manage to score a hit. Flight Lieutenant Lancey had his bomb hang up, overshot; then the bomb dropped away and crashed down the mountain side. When Grant Perry, his wireless operator, visited the area thirty-three years later, even at that late date, people still remember the attack that day in April 1945.

When the whole force had bombed, the barracks at Berchtesgaden had taken many hits. The north-west building was demolished and the remainder severely damaged. A quarter of the main control centre was demolished and the administration HQ set on fire. Hitler's number two residence, in which his guests usually stayed, was also severely damaged. Direct hits by 617 were scored on Hitler's Chalet. According to later records and intelligence, the fuses on the Tallboys were set for deep penetration. One of the fighter pilots later said, 'It was excellent bombing, the place was an inferno, smoke rising to 10,000 feet.'

Flying Officer Coster of 9 Squadron, said the barracks took a 'terrific pasting'. His mid-upper gunner, Morrison, saw the door of one building go flying through the air and fall on another building. He was later known as 'One Door Morrison'. Another pilot from Australia, Flying Officer Butler, said, 'There was a pall of smoke and dust all over the aiming points, the largest one being over the house but the whole area was straddled and even if Hitler was in the garden or nearby woods, I wouldn't like to be his insurance company.' Coster also remarked that if Hitler wasn't there this time he wouldn't mind going back again in the hope of catching him.

In the event they didn't have to. On 30th April Hitler committed suicide and the devastated Berghof was captured shortly afterwards by the 101st Airborne Division. A few days later the war was over.

CHAPTER SIXTEEN

The War is Over

In two years of war, 617 Squadron had attacked some 95 targets, the first the Ruhr Dams in May 1943 which gave them a unique place in history, the last against Hitler's lair, in April 1945. The rate worked out at about one target per week. Not as many as main force squadrons who might have been out several times in a week, but 617's operations were of a special type, usually requiring special treatment.

There were some targets that though not in fact attacked by 617 were proposed. In July 1943, Sir Arthur Harris had a plan to assassinate Mussolini, in his villa in Italy. Harris had hatched the plan in December 1942, but it was shelved after the Dams Raid; he re-introduced it, saying that the force would consist 'of my squadron of "Old Lags".' (617 Squadron). The villa was in Rome and at this time there was great difference of opinion about bombing Rome or the surrounding area, so the plan was eventually thrown out by Anthony Eden in July 1943. Another target not attacked was the Rothensee Ship lift which if destroyed, would have brought the waterways traffic between the Ruhr and the centre of Germany to a complete stop.

Although the bouncing bomb was invented and used on water it was also considered for use on land. On 10th June 1943 a test was made by two 617 Squadron aircraft at Ashley Walk Bombing Range. Two bouncing bombs were dropped from 100 feet at a speed of 230 mph and each bomb spun at 500 rpm. The first went 900 yards and the second 1,080 yards. The problem at this height was damage to the aircraft. One was peppered with small stones thrown up when the bomb hit the ground on each bounce. On the 9th a further test was made from 250 feet and 210 mph. The bombs went 500 and 640 yards, each bomb bounce made a crater about 3′ 6″ across. The report suggested a maximum height of drop as 150 feet but nothing was ever pursued along these lines.

The station at Woodhall Spa has virtually disappeared, most of it having been returned to the land. An odd mound of rubble which once had been a building, hangar or aircraft dispersal point, is all that is left. It seems hard to imagine the likes of Nick Knilans, Bob Knights and Willie Tait dragging their Lancasters into the air with their great 12,000-lb bombs under them, and later in 1945 the Lancasters taking off with the largest bomb of the war, the Grand Slam, or Leonard Cheshire taking off in his Mosquito or Mustang on many sorties to mark a target for the others.

The Petwood Hotel is still very much as it was in those days. Set in its beautiful grounds and gardens, it's a wonderful place to spend a weekend. The owners are very proud of its wartime associations. The hotel has its own squadron bar in which many 617 mementoes are kept; it even has a tyre of a Lancaster there. The pond is still there and one remembers Ian Ross fishing there, sadly to die later in the water off Norway. As one enters the Hotel, up the long drive, there is a sign telling visitors that this was once the wartime Officers' Mess of 617 Squadron.

In May 1945 Operation Exodus was put in motion, conveying former prisoners of war from Europe, home to the UK. The POWs were assembled at suitable airfields on the Continent from which they were to be flown back to Britain. They were given a tremendous reception. At one station alone, over half a ton of cake was eaten and 15,000 cups of tea drunk.

No 617 started Exodus on 8th May (VE day) flying to Brussels via a staging point at Juvincourt. These flights continued until the 14th. The next day two flights went to view the damage in a low level flight to and from Woodhall, covering the Frisians, Heligoland, Hamburg, Brunswick, Hanover, Bielefeld viaduct, the Dortmund-Ems Canal, Cologne and other former targets. These were to show some of the ground personnel what their aircrews had done and had achieved – but only achieved with their help and support.

On the 29th, part of 617 Squadron were detached to RAF

Mildenhall as 'C' Flight of 15 Squadron under the command of Wing Commander Jock Calder. Maybe as the result of VE Day celebrations, beer became very short in May-June 1945. Due to this the bar at Mildenhall was closed quite early each day. To combat this sad state of affairs, 617 types would order a large jug of beer before closing time. As the beer then became even more scarce, and the station were hoping to hold a summer ball and wanted to conserve stocks, 617 were nearly banned from the Mess totally.

Meanwhile, the squadron had been selected by Bomber Command HQ to become part of Tiger Force. This force was to operate in the Far East against the Japanese. The destination was Chittagong. Much training in the months of June to August took place in preparation for this event, at RAF Waddington. However, the ending of the war against Japan cancelled this project.

In September, the squadron were involved in Operation Dodge, which brought former prisoners of war home to England from Italy and while this went on, more sight-seeing flights were made, this time to Berlin.

Then in January 1946, the squadron, along with its old friendly rivals, 9 Squadron, were sent to India, ending up at Digri; 9 was based at an adjacent field at Salbani. The Indian Navy had mutinied at Bombay and all aircraft were armed with masses of .5 ammunition in all turrets in case they were needed to quell the mutiny. Happily it was put down before 617 were needed. While in India, 617 took part in the Delhi Air Show, in April 1946, attended by Lord Wavell, the viceroy.

In 1946, 617 were back in England, at RAF Binbrook and from there it left for a goodwill tour of Canada in July and later to the USA returning in September. By now the squadron was flying the new Lincoln aircraft. Its CO was Wing Commander G.D. Milne, DFC and the two flight commanders were Squadron Leaders C.K. Saxelby, DFC and A.G. Lang, DFC.

In 1950, 617 were awarded the Laurence Minot trophy by the King at Buckingham Palace. The trophy had been presented to the RAF in 1926 in memory of Captain Laurence Minot, MC who had been killed in action in 1917 while serving with 57 Squadron RFC. It was awarded to the best pilot and bomb aimer in competition with other bomber squadrons. Among the names already on the trophy was Wing Commander 'Peter' Portal, later Viscount Portal. He had won it while with 7 Squadron. They won it seven times up to 1936, sharing it on one occasion with 58 Squadron, commanded by Wing Commander Arthur Harris! In the final, 617 competed against 214 Squadron.

The squadron became part of the new jet age in 1952 when it equipped with the Canberra light bomber, then in 1955 the squadron again went overseas, this time to Malaya for operations against Communist terrorists. On 15th December 1955 they were disbanded, but were reformed in May 1958 at Scampton, its original birthplace. It became the first squadron to fly the Vulcan bomber.

The squadron received its standard on 14th May 1959, presented by Queen Elizabeth, the Queen Mother. The standard, showing all its many battle honours, was granted in 1952 but not presented till seven years later.

Over the years the squadron took part in many events associated with a peacetime air force, fully prepared for war. On 21st June 1961, one of its Vulcans flew non-stop from England to Australia (XH481) piloted by Squadron Leader M.G. Bearis. The 11,500 mile trip took 20 hours 3 minutes at an average speed of 573 mph. In February 1963 617 were in full training with the, then new, Blue Steel missiles.

In December 1981, while the squadron was still operating with the Vulcan, the aircraft described as having no vices, a flight was arranged over the Lady Bower reservoir and the Derwent Dam in Derbyshire, which had been used by 617 in practising for the Dams Raid in 1943. The aircraft flown by Wing Commandr Herbertson (in XL318) was dismantled after this flight, and taken by road to Hendon in north London, to reside in the new Bomber Command Museum there.

Once again the squadron was disbanded – in December 1981, but only for twelve months. On 1st January 1983 it was reformed with the new Tornado which costs 12 million pounds to build, compared with 20,000 pounds for a Lancaster. It has a slightly different title – 617 Tornado Squadron – and it is based at RAF Marham in Norfolk and will have sixteen aircraft when at full strength. The new CO, Wing Commander Tony Harrison, is a pilot, and very keen on the name and famous background of his squadron. He is very proud of being given such a command and his son, in keeping up the tradition, is at the moment swatting for his 'O' levels. One subject he is writing about is, yes, 617 Squadron and the Dams Raid.

In 1983 the squadron celebrates its fortieth anniversary of the Dams Raid and with, now only about thirty-five survivors of that raid, they are going to make sure the event does not go unnoticed. There was a dinner on the night of 16th May, at Marham, with not only the survivors of the raid but many post-Dams crew members from all over the world. There were other events in the Lincoln area, and a service at Lincoln Cathedral on the 16th in memory of the 184 men of the squadron who lost their lives while flying with the squadron. Lincoln Cathedral is of course, very close to many a crew's heart, for those who operated from the surrounding countryside, it was a very prominent feature on the landscape for returning crews.

The aircraft have changed over the years but the spirit of the men who fly them has not. In forty years the men of the RAF and of 617 Squadron are still very similar in outlook. Values may change but the spirit of the men who flew them and who fly now remains unchanged. In 1943 they became known as the Dambusters, but as this book has shown, the squadron achieved much more after the famous event.

The motto of the Royal Air Force is *Per Ardua ad Astra* – 'Through Hardship to the Stars'. In writing this book I have understood their hardships, I would have liked to have seen the stars with them.

Sources

617 Personnel

Norman Baty
Chris Cole
P.W. Derham DFC
B. Forshaw
Bill Harris
Sidney Hobday DFC
Charles Housten DFC
Gus Hoyland
Reg Petch DFC
Ron Pooley DFM
Nicky Ross DSO DFC
Jim Thompson
Ron Valentine
Don Cheney DFC
Basil Fish
G. Alex Phillys
R. Hunnisett
A.N. Fearn DFC
S. Harris
T. Payne
Dave Rodger DFC
T.J. McLean DFC DFM
Jack Hager
J.H. Brook
R. Blagden
Mick Chamberlain
Bill Reid VC
E. Weaver
Bill Howarth DFM
J.M. Chapman
Mark Flatman
Donald Bell DFC
Nick Knilans DSO DFC
Keith Astbury DFC
Charlie Wiltshire
John Flynn

S/L W.H. Gordon MBE DFC
Jack Forshaw
Ian Marshall DFM
Jim Heveron
G.H. Riley
Arthur Joplin
Bobby Knights DSO DFC
Frank Tilley
Gerry Hobbs
Edwin Baldwin
Freddie Watts DFC
James Thompson
Harold Riding
Bob Barry
D.H. Maclennan
Gerry Witherick DFC DFM
J. Penswick
J. Blagbrough DFM
F.E. Hawkins
Paddy Gingles DFC DFM
W.S. Richardson
Grant Perry
B.J.D. Bird
Loftus Hebbard
J.H. Jones
S/L Hugh Brown
Terry Playford DFC
Frank Cardwell
C.B. Crafer DFC
G. Matthews
J. Merchant
R. Learmouth DFM
W. Rupert
P. Whitaker
A.S. Bates
S.J. Henderson

G. Irwin
S/L E.A. Wass
Albert Hepworth
R. Henderson
T. Brand
A. Dicken DFC
K. Stretch
Lloyd Pinder
Dennis Cooper
Alex Sharp
Tony Iveson DFC
Harry Farino
Joe Dacey DFC
G/Capt Leonard Cheshire
   VC OM DSO DFC
George 'Chiefy' Powell
Air Marshal Sir Harold Martin KCB
   DSO DFC AFC
G/Captain Hamish Mahaddie DSO
   DFC AFC
Ernie Twells DFC
Bill Carey DFC
Dickie Willsher DFC
F.J. Gorringe DSO
W.H. Kellaway DSO
Bernard Kent DFC
J.L. Sayers DFC

Next of Kin
Georgina Bramber (née Maltby)
Pauline Judge
Lily R. Williams
Mrs P. Jones
Brian J. Skinner
Mrs D.J. Finch
Mrs V.D. Peck
Mrs D. Long
Mr J. Trefar Thomas
Geoffrey Allsebrook
Herb Weeden
Jane Buckley (née Allsebrook)
Marshal Of The Royal Air Force
Sir Arthur T. Harris BT GCB OBE
   AFC
The Hon Sir Ralph A Cochrane GCB
   CBE DSO DFC AFC

General
Dr R.M.S. Matthews
H.W. Pride
C. Spalding 9 Sqdn
J. Hall
BBC TV (Edward Mirzeoff)
R.W. Board DFC (463 Sqdn)
B.A. Buckham DSO DFC (463 Sqdn)
Group Capt C.N. Bilney
R.S. Humphreys
Danny Boon
W/C R.G.W. Oakley DSO DFC AFC
   DFM (627 Sqdn)
L.W. Langley (9 Sqdn)
A.L. Fuller
Peter Sharpe
I.A. Gillender
David Hamilton
K. Llewelyn RAAF Public Relations
   Officer
Kay Rowland
Group Capt Eric McCabe
W/C Wally Dunn OBE
F/Lt G.H. Capsey
G. Briggs
Miss Susan Digges
Raymond P. Hepner
C. Simpson
Tony Landeg
George Scutt
A.W.H. Cheffins Pilot & Observers
   Ass., Winnipeg
Don Dearn
Stan Richmond
Gordon Musgrove DFC & BAR
Ralph Barker
Alfred Price
Martin Middlebrook
Ray Harris DFC 9 Sqdn
Ed Stowell DFC 9 Sqdn
Dave Coster 9 Sqdn
Sir Barnes Wallis
A.H. Horry 9 Sqdn
R. Harvey 9 Sqdn
L.G.A. Hadland 9 Sqdn
S/L Bill William DFC 9 Sqdn
L.W. Langley 9 Sqdn
J.C. Pinning 9 Sqdn

Alex Ritchie 9 Sqdn
Phil Tetlow 9 Sqdn
A. Whitworth 9 Sqdn
P.A. Morgan 9 Sqdn
G.H. Irwin 9 Sqdn
J. Wiley 9 Sqdn
L.C. Westrope 9 Sqdn
W. Andrews 9 Sqdn
K. Mallinson 9 Sqdn
W. Gregory 9 Sqdn
D. Nolan 9 Sqdn
E. Selfe 9 Sqdn
G. Hopgood 9 Sqdn
B. Taylor 9 Sqdn
W. Gabriel DFC 9 Sqdn
W/C K. Lewis DFC 9 Sqdn
J. Gold 9 Sqdn
L. Marsh 9 Sqdn
P.H. Jones 9 Sqdn
R. Lake 9 Sqdn
J. Foot 9 Sqdn
J. Parsons 9 Sqdn
J. Singer DFC 9 Sqdn
F. Millington 9 Sqdn
P. Tetlow 9 Sqdn
Bob Gardiner
Robert Cockburn
E. Shields DFC Sqdn
D. Richards
G.C. Adams
N.H. Prowting
Peter Cornish
George Griffiths DFM
Pat Dryden
S.D. Boyd
Frank Hawkins
Doris Howarth
Diana Birch
Hildegard Gaze
  (for her help in translation work)
Jeremy Hall
Stuart Stephenson (Lincolnshire Lan-
  caster Committee)

Newspapers
Sunday Express
Daily Express
Nordlys Tromso
Daily Telegraph
Lincoln Echo
Norfolk & Suffolk Aviation Museum
NSD Flyg-Extra Sweden
'Bergens Tidende'
L'Indépandant (St Omer) France
The Times
South Wales Argus (Anne Jones)

Magazines
Flypast
After the Battle
Air Mail (RAF Association)

Other Sources
Instruments of Darkness, Alfred Price
The Tirpitz Incident, J.A.G. Werner &
  Girbig
Menace The Life and Death of the Tirpitz,
  Ludovic Kennedy
Bergen In War, Tim Greve
Lancaster in Lapland, John Bryggman
  and Rume Tannersjo
Flying Review International, Flyghist
  Revy
The Chance of Tirpitz, Gunnar Pedersen
Sink the Tirpitz, Leonce Peillard

Official Sources
MOD RAF Records Gloucester
Commonwealth War Graves
MOD AR9 (Mrs Elderfield)
London Gazette
Air Historical Branch (G/Capt Probert
  Mr Munday)
Public Record Office, Kew
617 Sqdn Association, Tony Iveson
  DFC
617 Sqdn Association (Canada), Don
  Bell
Bomber Commd Re-union Association
  (Ray Callow)
Bomber Commd Association (Harry
  Pitcher, Bill Rust)
Aircrew Association
Air Gunners Association
RAF Prisoners of War Association
RAF Escaping Society

617 Sqdn RAF Marham
9 Sqdn RAF Honington
9 Sqdn Association – Jim Brookbank
British Aerospace – Manchester
   Division
Gemeinde Ladbergen
Gemeente Denham
Stadt Nordhorn
Ministry of Defence (New Zealand)
Kreispolizeibehörde in Kleve
Polizeistation Emmerich
RAF Museum, Hendon
Australian War Memorial Museum
Bomber Command Association (NZ
   Section)
Imperial War Museum
   Dept of Film (Queenie Turner)
   Dept of Photographs (Ted Hine)

Foreign
André Schamp
Magne Endal
G. Rickertser
Gerhard Bracke
Herr Willibald Völsing
Mauritz Erikson
Knut M. Haugland
Norges Hjemmefront Museum, Oslo
Lars Thoring
Johannes Ullrich
Hans Magnus Hansen

Captain Bernhard Schmitz
Björn Rosenberger
Ragnar Kvalstad
Kaare Johnsen
Leif-Erik Simonsen
Mrs Tordis Rying
Arnold Olsen
Egil Akre
Jens Olsen Tennskjer
Helge Richardsen
Jost W. Schneider
Georg Schwallbach
Hans-Ludwig Bortfeldt
Pier Skaugstad
Herr Böttcher, Town Hall, Syke
Ole Saclensminde
Jan Hjornevik
Tor Kaasam
Kaye Weedon
J. Eefting
Tom Kasper Olsen
H.B. Van Helden
L. Zwaaf Jr
Bjorn Olsen
Administration Communale, de
   Merbes-Le-Chateau
Norbert Kruger
D.S. Drijver
Horst Muller, for all his great support
Singolf Sjvisnes
Ruth & Olviend Talil

Public Records Office
References

Air 27 -2128
Air 27 - 2129
Air 27 - 1922
Air 27 - 1701
Air 27 - 2007
Air 27 - 578
Air 14 - 2691
Air 14 - 3559
Air 14 - 2234
Air 14 - 3033
Air 14 - 548
Air 14 - 1864
Air 14 - 3458
Air 14 - 2188
Air 14 - 2007
Air 14 - 1975
Air 14 - 1972
Air 14 - 2226
Air 14 - 3453
Air 14 - 715
Air 14 - 3875
Air 14 - 3876
Air 14 - 1962
Air 14 - 2222
Air 14 - 2051
Air 14 - 731
Air 14 - 2073
Air 14 - 2229
Air 14 - 2323
Air 14 - 3378
Air 14 - 2042

Air 14 - 2534
Air 14 - 2224
Air 14 - 1976
Air 14 - 2127
Air 14 - 2007
Air 14 - 2023
Air 14 - 2035
Air 14 - 1999
Air 14 - 1971 to 1977
Air 14 - 1111
Air 14 - 994
Air 14 - 868
Air 14 - 2226
Air 14 - 1666
Air 14 - 2040
Air 11 - 2328
Air 14 - 717
Air 14 - 2534
Air 14 - 2180
Air 14 - 3377
Air 14 - 2223
Air 24 - 206
Air 24 - 207
Air 24 - 310
Air 24 - 308
Air 24 - 283
Air 24 - 292
Air 24 - 268
Air 24 - 1734
Air 24 - 298
Air 24 - 303

Air 24 - 5109
Air 24 - 272
Air 24 - 290
Air 27 - 128
Air 41 - 43
Air 34 - 678
Air 34 - 141
Air 34 - 673
Air 34 - 676
Air 40 - 2015
Air 40 - 1247
Air 40 - 1248
Air 40 - 2015
Air 40 - 1699
Air 40 - 1762
Air 29 - 854
Air 20 - 798
Air 20 - 2279
Air 20 - 5776
Air 20 - 5321
Air 20 - 5321
Air 20 - 1059
Air 20 - 1097
Air 20 - 7709
Air 48 - 128
Air 48 - 119
Air 48 - 115
Air 48 - 112
Air 48 - 111
Air 28 - 786
Air 4 - 37

Air 4 - 48
Air 20 - 1215
Air 20 - 1309
Air 20 - 2682
Air 20 - 6187
Air 20 - 822
Air 10 - 4039
Air 10 - 4038
Air 50 - 205
Avia 18 - 917
Adm 1 - 16699
Prem 3 - 191/1
Cab 69 - 5
Adm 223 - 88
Adm 223 - 87
Adm 223 - 51
Air 24 - 1582
Air 24 - 291
Air 24 - 280
Air 24 - 281
Air 2 - 10344
Air 2 - 5444
Air 2 - 2323
Defe 2 - 307
Air 25 - 110
Air 25 - 124
WO 205 - 1053
WO 208
Air 30
Air 2 Code 30
London Gazette
   Honours and Awards

Appendices

Appendix I

617 Squadron Song

The Möhne and Eder Dams were standing in the Ruhr,
Till 617 Squadron came and knocked them to the floor,
But since that operation the squadron's been a flop,
For they've got the reputation of the squadron with one op.
     Come and join us etc.

Selected for the squadron they were the finest crews,
But the only thing they're good for is going on the booze,
They don't care for Jerry and they don't care for Wops,
For they only go to Boston to do their blooming ops.
     Come and join us etc.

The Main Force of the Air Force who put Berlin through the mill,
Want to come to 617 to get a real big thrill,
No sooner they reach Woodhall they find that they've done wrong,
For the only thing they get here is another NAAFI gong.
     Come and join us etc.

Now all you budding aircrews who don't want to go to Heaven,
Want to come and join the forces of good old 617,
The Main Force go to Berlin and are fighting their way back,
While our boys go to Wainfleet where there isn't any flak.
     Come and join us etc.

Now the crews we have at Woodhall are as famous as the rest,
For they went and sank the *Tirpitz* and the UBoat pens at Brest,
They went to see Joe Stalin and they thought they'd sleep on rugs,
But out there in their billets they got bitten to death by bugs.
     Come and join us etc.

The ground crews of the squadron are the finest lads we've known,
They serviced Gibson's Lankies for the Dam raids as you know,
They gave them three days holiday they said it was enough,
But since that operation they've been treated blinking rough.
     Come and join us etc.

617 Squadron and the Tirpitz

Among those fields rich with corn
Clear on a cool summer's morn
The clustered hangers of Woodhall stand
Green walled in the trees of bomber land
Around about them airfield sweep
Lancs in dispersal fruited deep
As fair as the garden of the Lord
In the eyes of that squadron hoard
Twenty Lancs with petrol stowed
Twenty Lancs with a tallboy load
All ready in the morning sun
But the noon day saw not one
Higher rose six one seven's men
Bowed with their early teens plus ten
Taking up that late summer's task
What of us all bomber Harris did ask
Down the track came the marauding throng
Willie Tirpitz Tait leading along
Under that slouched hat far to the right
Tirpitz the target met his sight
On went the dusty blue ranks so fast
Down went the bombs – up went the blast
Shoot if you must this young grey head
But spare your country's navy he said
To humbler nature within them stirred
To life at that squadron's deed and word
Who touches a hair of one Norwegian head
Dies like a dog – fly on he said.

John Pryor, DFC.

176

Appendix II

617 Squadron Targets

The Dams	16/17 May 1943
Aquata Scriva (Italy)	15/17 July 1943
San Polo D'Enza	15/17 July 1943
Leghorn (Italy)	24 July 1943
Milan (Italy)	29 July 1943
Turin (Italy)	29 July 1943
Genoa (Italy)	29 July 1943
Bologna (Italy)	29 July 1943
Dortmund Ems Canal	15 September 1943
Antheor Viaduct	16 September 1943
Antheor Viaduct	11 November 1943
Flixecourt	16 December 1943
Liege	20 December 1943
Pas De Calais	22 December 1943
Flixecourt	31 December 1943
Pas De Calais	14 January 1944
Pas De Calais	21 January 1944
Pas De Calais	25 January 1944
Limoges	8 February 1944
Antheor Viaduct	12 February 1944
Albert	2 March 1944
St Etienne	4 March 1944
St Etienne	10 March 1944
Woippy	15 March 1944
Clermont Ferrand	16 March 1944
Bergerac	18 March 1944
Angouleme	20 March 1944
Lyons	23 March 1944
Lyons	25 March 1944
Lyons	29 March 1944
Toulouse	5 April 1944
St Cyr	10 April 1944
Juvisy	18 April 1944
Juvisy	20 April 1944
Brunswick	22 April 1944

Munich	24 April 1944
Milan	24 April 1944
Mailly Camp	3 May 1944
D-Day Spoof	5 June 1944
Saumar Tunnel	8 June 1944
Le Havre	14 June 1944
Boulogne	15 June 1944
Watten	19 June 1944
Wizernes	20 June 1944
Wizernes	22 June 1944
Wizernes	24 June 1944
Siracourt	25 June 1944
Creil	4 July 1944
Mimoyecques	6 July 1944
Wizernes	17 July 1944
Wizernes	20 July 1944
Watten	25 July 1944
Rilly La Montagne	31 July 1944
Siracourt	1 August 1944
Etaples	4 August 1944
Brest	5 August 1944
Keroman (Ship)	6 August 1944
Lorient	7 August 1944
La Pallice	9 August 1944
La Pallice	11 August 1944
Brest	12 August 1944
Gueydon (Ship) Brest	13 August 1944
Gueydon (Ship) Brest	14 August 1944
La Pallice	16 August 1944
La Pallice	18 August 1944
Ijmuiden	24 August 1944
Brest	27 August 1944
Tirpitz (Ship)	11 September 1944
Dortmund Ems Canal	23 September 1944
Westkappel Sea Wall	3 October 1944
Kembs Canal	7 October 1944
Tirpitz (Ship)	29 October 1944
Tirpitz (Ship)	12 November 1944
Urft Dam	8 December 1944
Urft Dam	11 December 1944
Ijmuiden	15 December 1944
Politz	21 December 1944
Rotterdam	29 December 1944
Ijmuiden	30 December 1944
Oslo (Shipping) 31/1 January 1945	
Bergen (Norway)	12 January 1945
Poortershaven	3 February 1945
Bielefeld	6 February 1945
Ijmuiden	8 February 1945

Bielefeld	14 February 1945
Bielefeld	22 February 1945
Dortmund-Ems Canal	24 February 1945
Bielefeld	13 March 1945
Bielefeld	14 March 1945
Arnsberg	15 March 1945
Arnsberg	19 March 1945
Dreys	21 March 1945
Nienburg	23 March 1945
Farge	27 March 1945
Ijmuiden	6 April 1945
Ijmuiden	7 April 1945
Hamburg U-Boat Pens	9 April 1945
Prinz Eugen/Lutzow (Ships)	13 April 1945
Lützow (Ship)	15 April 1945
Lützow (Ship)	16 April 1945
Heligoland	19 April 1945
Berchtesgarden	25 April 1945

Total of operations between May 1943 and April 1945 – 95.

Appendix III

Roll of Honour

P/O John Fort	RAF	14th September 1943
Sgt William Hatton	RAF	14th September 1943
F/S Victor Hill	RAF	14th September 1943
S/L David John Hatfield Maltby, DSO	RAF	14th September 1943
F/S Vivian Nicholson, DFM	RAF	14th September 1943
Sgt Harold Thomas Simmons	RAF	14th September 1943
F/S Anthony Joseph Stone	RAF	14th September 1943
Sgt David Allatson	RAF	16th September 1943
F/Lt Athelsie Pole Allsebrook, DSO, DFC	RAF	16th September 1943
Sgt Ernest Cecil Allan Blake	RAF	16th September 1943
PO Norman Arthur Botting, DFC	RAF	16th September 1943
F/O George Henry Coles	RCAF	16th September 1943
F/S George Andrew Deering, DFC	RAF	16th September 1943
F/O William George Divall	RAF	16th September 1943
F/O Jacob Maurice Grant, DFC	RAF	16th September 1943
F/S Samuel Hitchen	RAF	16th September 1943
W/C George Walton Holden, DSO, DFC & Bar MID	RAF	16th September 1943
F/S Eric Hornby	RAF	16th September 1943
F/Lt Robert Edward George Hutchinson, DFC & Bar	RAF	16th September 1943
P/O Thomas William Johnson	RAF	16th September 1943
Sgt Ivor Glyn Jones	RAF	16th September 1943
F/Lt Leslie Gordon Knight, DSO, MID (Post)	RAF	16th September 1943
Sgt Clifford Morrell Knox	RAF	16th September 1943
F/S Reginald Bertram Sidney Lulham	RAF	16th September 1943
F/S Robert Campbell McArthur	RAF	16th September 1943
P/O Thomas Alfred Meikle, DFM	RAF	16th September 1943
WO Lloyd Mieyette	RCAF	16th September 1943
P/O Gernald Stanley Miles	RAF	16th September 1943
F/Lt Phillip Moore	RAF	16th September 1943
F/S Trevor Herrington Payne	RAF	16th September 1943
F/S Dean John Powell, MID	RAF	16th September 1943
F/O Henry Thomas Hames Pringle, DFC	RAF	16th September 1943
F/O James Alexander Rodger	RAF	16th September 1943

F/S James Stevenson Simpson	RAF	16th September 1943
F/O Frederick Michael Spafford, DFC, DFM	RAF	16th September 1943
F/Lt Tonger Harlo Taerum, DFC	RCAF	16th September 1943
F/S William Walker	RAF	16th September 1943
F/O Douglas William Warwick	RCAF	16th September 1943
Sgt Austin Ainsworth Williams	RAF	16th September 1943
F/Lt Harold Sydney Wilson	RAF	16th September 1943
F/S Ronald Florence, DFM	RNAF	18th November 1943
F/O Walter Crawford Grimes, DFM	RAF	18th November 1943
P/O Alan MacBeilly Laughland, DFM	RCAF	18th November 1943
WO John Brian De Courcy O'Grady	RCAF	18th November 1943
P/O Leonard Plishka	RCAF	18th November 1943
P/O Sam James Whittingham, DFC	RAF	18th November 1943
F/Lt Edward Ernest George Youseman, DFC	RAF	18th November 1943
WO Robert Cummings	RCAF	10th December 1943
F/S Robert Geoffrey Howell	RAF	10th December 1943
P/O Ralph Neville Jones	RAF	10th December 1943
Sgt Arthur William Richardson	RAF	10th December 1943
Sgt Brook Robinson	RAF	10th December 1943
Sgt John McLean Stewart	RAF	10th December 1943
WO Donald Menzies Thorpe	RCAF	10th December 1943
F/O Gordon Herbert Weeden	RCAF	10th December 1943
Sgt Stephen Burns	RAF	20th December 1943
Sgt Chester Bruce Gowrie	RCAF	20th December 1943
F/O Richard MacFarlane	RAF	20th December 1943
Sgt Thomas William Maynard	RAF	20th December 1943
Sgt Edward Clarence Smith	RAF	20th December 1943
F/O John William Thrasher	RCAF	20th December 1943
F/Lt Arthur David Holding	RAF	20th January 1944
F/Lt Thomas Vincent O'Shaughnessy	RAF	20th January 1944
F/Lt Robert Claude Hay, DFC & Bar	RAAF	12th February 1944
F/O Norman James Davidson	RCAF	13th February 1944
F/O John McBride Dempster, DFM	RCAF	13th February 1944
F/O John Irvine Gordon, DFC	RAAF	13th February 1944
Sgt John Pulford, DFM	RAF	13th February 1944
F/S John Paul Riches	RAF	13th February 1944
S/L William Suggitt, DFC	RCAF	15th February 1944
F/O George James Harden, DFC	RAF	24th April 1944
F/Lt John Andrew Edward, DFC	RAF	24th June 1944
F/S Samuel Isherwood	RAF	24th June 1944
F/O James Ian Johnstone, DFC	RCAF	24th June 1944
F/O Leslie William John King, DFC, MID	RAF	24th June 1944
WO Thomas William Percy Price	RAF	24th June 1944
F/S Albert Arthur Holt	RAF	31st July 1944
WO John Williams Hutton, DFC	RAF	31st July 1944
F/O Joseph Ovila Peltier	RCAF	31st July 1944
F/O Leslie George Rolton, DFC	RAF	31st July 1944
F/S Donald George William Stewart	RAF	31st July 1944
F/S Reginald Howard Pool	RAF	5th August 1944

P/O William Noel Wait	RAF	5th August 1944
P/O Robert Welch	RAF	5th August 1944
F/Lt Warren Alvin Duffy	RCAF	7th August 1944
F/O Philip Ingleby	RAF	7th August 1944
F/O Cecil Percy Pesme	RCAF	14th August 1944
F/O Charles Lawrence Fox	RAF	17th September 1944
Sgt Peter William Groom	RAF	17th September 1944
F/O Frank Levy	RAF	17th September 1944
F/S George Muir McGuire	RAF	17th September 1944
F/O Allan Frank McNally	RCAF	17th September 1944
F/O James Fraser Naylor	RAF	17th September 1944
F/S Eric Edward Stephen Peck	RAF	17th September 1944
F/O Charles Shea	RAF	17th September 1944
F/S Daniel Goronwy Thomas	RAF	17th September 1944
P/O Alan William Benting	RAF	23rd September 1944
F/O Clive Evans Miles Graham, MID	RAF	23rd September 1944
F/Lt Geoffrey Stevenson Stout, DFC	RAF	23rd September 1944
F/O George Edward Cansell	RAF	7th October 1944
F/S Herbert George Clarke, MID	RAF	7th October 1944
P/O Eric Albert Hartley	RAF	7th October 1944
P/O Frederick Charles Hawkins	RAF	7th October 1944
F/O Herbert Walter Honig	RAF	7th October 1944
F/Lt Thomas Horricks	RAF	7th October 1944
F/O Bruce James Hosie	RAF	7th October 1944
F/Lt Christopher John Howard	RAF	7th October 1944
F/Lt Thomas James Hurdiss	RAF	7th October 1944
P/O Richard Dennis Lucan	RAF	7th October 1944
F/Lt Thomas Jobson Tate	RAF	7th October 1944
F/O David Trevor Watkins, DFC	RAF	7th October 1944
F/Lt Ronald Henry Williams, DFC	RAF	7th October 1944
WO Philip Edwin Woods	RAF	7th October 1944
S/L Drew Rothwell Cullen Wyness, DFC	RAF	7th October 1944
F/O Arthur James Walker, DFC	RAF	21st December 1944
F/O Robertson Bertram Yates	RAF	21st December 1944
WO Sydney Ross Anderson	RAF	12th January 1945
F/O Mowbray Ellwood, DFM	RAF	12th January 1945
F/S Leslie Douglas Griffiths	RAF	12th January 1945
P/O George Alfred Kendrick	RAF	12th January 1945
F/O Alexander Farley Mckellow	RAF	12th January 1945
F/O Ian Steward Ross	RAAF	12th January 1945
F/O Edward George Tilby	RAF	12th January 1945
F/S William Walter	RAF	12th January 1945
F/O Edwin Alfred Barnett	RAF	21st March 1945
F/O George Bell	RAF	21st March 1945
F/O Kenneth Gill, DFC, C de G	RAF	21st March 1945
F/Lt Bernard Alexander Gumbley, DFM	RNAF	21st March 1945
F/Lt Joseph Charles Randon	RAF	21st March 1945
F/Lt Michael Ternce Clarke, DFC	RAF	16th April 1945
F/S Henry William Felton, DFM	RAF	16th April 1945

F/O Alfred Lawrence Heath	RAF	16th April 1945
P/O Kenneth Arthur John Hewitt	RAF	16th April 1945
P/O William Knight	RAF	16th April 1945
S/L John Leonard Powell, DFC	RAF	16th April 1945
F/O James Watson	RAF	16th April 1945

Total killed: 189 This includes the 53 killed on the Dams Raid, see *The Men Who Breached the Dams*, published Wm. Kimber & Co. 1982.

Appendix IV

Victoria Cross

W/C G.L. Cheshire	617 Sqdn London Gazette 8/9/1944
A/F/Lt W. Reid	61 Sqdn London Gazette 14/12/1943

Distinguished Service Order

F/Lt R.A.P. Allesbrook	49 Sqdn London Gazette 9/7/1943
A/W/C C.C. Calder	158 Sqdn London Gazette 13/6/1944
F/O K. Castagnola	617 Sqdn London Gazette 26/10/1945
F/O G.L. Cheshire	102 Sqdn London Gazette 6/12/1940
A/F/Lt B.W. Clayton	617 Sqdn London Gazette 26/9/1944
S/L G.B. Ellwood	405 Sqdn London Gazette 29/9/1944
A/W/C J.E. Fauquier	405 Sqdn London Gazette 17/9/1943
A/S/L G.E. Fawke	617 Sqdn London Gazette 2/1/1945
F/Lt F.J. Gorringe	617 Sqdn London Gazette 21/9/1945
A/W/C G.W. Holden	102 Sqdn London Gazette 11/6/1943
A/F/Lt R.S.D. Kearns	617 Sqdn London Gazette 26/9/1944
A/F/Lt W.H. Kellaway	149 Sqdn London Gazette 30/3/1943
A/F/Lt R.E. Knights	617 Sqdn London Gazette 12/1/1945
1st/Lt H.C. Knilans (USA)	619 Sqdn Approved 17/1/1943
A/S/L A.R. Poole	83 Sqdn London Gazette 21/9/45
F/O N.R. Ross	617 Sqdn London Gazette 29/8/1944
F/Lt J. Tait	51 Sqdn London Gazette 18/4/1941
A/S/L D.J.B. Wilson	617 Sqdn London Gazette 28/11/1944

Bar to Distinguished Service Order

W/C C.C. Calder	617 Sqdn London Gazette 5/6/1945
A/W/C G.L. Cheshire	76 Sqdn London Gazette 20/4/1943
G/Capt J.E. Fauquier	405 Sqdn London Gazette 31/3/1944
A/F/Lt W.H. Kellaway	630 Sqdn London Gazette 9/5/1944
S/L J.B. Tait	35 Sqdn London Gazette 25/7/1941

Second Bar to Distinguished Service Order

W/C G.L. Cheshire	617 Sqdn London Gazette 18/4/1944
G/Capt J.E. Fauquier	617 Sqdn London Gazette 1/6/1945
W/C J.B. Tait	617 Sqdn London Gazette 22/9/1944

W/C J.B. Tait   617 Sqdn London Gazette 9/1/1945

Distinguished Flying Cross

F/O R. Adams	617 Sqdn London Gazette 30/6/1944
P/O R.J. Allen	196 Sqdn London Gazette 19/10/1943
F/O R.A.P. Allesbrook	49 Sqdn London Gazette 14/4/1942
A/F/Lt S.A. Anning	44 Sqdn London Gazette 14/2/1945
F/O C.K. Astbury	49 Sqdn London Gazette 14/5/1943
F/O D.W. Bale	617 Sqdn London Gazette 7/11/1943
P/O W.J.M.L. Barclay	156 Sqdn London Gazette 14/5/1943
A/F/Lt D.A. Bell	617 Sqdn London Gazette 13/10/1944
P/O J.R. Bell	617 Sqdn London Gazette 17/10/1944
F/Lt J.H. Benison	10 Sqdn London Gazette 23/3/1945
W/O W.T. Bennett	617 Sqdn London Gazette 23/5/1944
W/O N.R. Botting	49 Sqdn London Gazette 18/5/1943
A/F/Lt A.D.D. Brian	189 Sqdn London Gazette 21/9/1945
P/O J.F. Brookes	103 Sqdn London Gazette 4/8/1942
F/O P.W. Buttle	619 Sqdn London Gazette 27/6/1944
A/F/L C.C. Calder	76 Sqdn London Gazette 13/2/1942
F/O D.W. Carey	617 Sqdn London Gazette 23/3/1945
F/O J. Castagnola	57 Sqdn London Gazette 17/11/1944
F/O H.H. Chadwick	57 Sqdn London Gazette 23/5/1944
A/F/Lt E.B. Chandler	49 Sqdn London Gazette 15/10/1943
F/O D.H. Cheney	617 Sqdn London Gazette 16/1/1945
F/O G.L. Cheshire	102 Sqdn London Gazette 7/3/1941
F/O M.T. Clarke	57 Sqdn London Gazette 16/1/1945
F/O S.R. Clarke	617 Sqdn London Gazette 15/9/1944
F/O T.W. Clarkson	617 Sqdn London Gazette 21/12/1945
W/O B.W. Clayton	51 Sqdn London Gazette 20/4/1943
P/O J.V. Cockshott	61 Sqdn London Gazette 14/5/1943
P/O J.H. Cole	50 Sqdn London Gazette 19/9/1943
P/O J.L. Cooper	106 Sqdn London Gazette 14/1/1943
F/Lt C.B. Crafer	10 Sqdn London Gazette 23/3/1945
P/O L.W. Curtis	158 Sqdn London Gazette 17/8/1943
W/O J. Dacey	617 Sqdn London Gazette 30/6/1944
F/O W.A. Daniel	617 Sqdn London Gazette 5/12/1944
P/O T. Davies	57 Sqdn London Gazette 2/6/1944
F/O T.R. Davies	103 Sqdn London Gazette 13/10/1944
P/O A. Dicken	44 Sqdn London Gazette 17/10/1944
F/Lt B.J. Dobson	44 Sqdn London Gazette 17/10/1944
F/O F.E. Drew	106 Sqdn London Gazette 12/3/1943
F/O W.A. Duffy	617 Sqdn London Gazette 22/8/1944
A/F/LT J.A. Edward	50 Sqdn London Gazette 11/2/1944
W/O H. Ellis	83 Sqdn London Gazette 25/5/1945
F/O G.B. Ellwood	405 Sqdn London Gazette 15/10/1943
F/O R.J. Elsey	106 Sqdn London Gazette 2/6/1944
P/O N. Evans	617 Sqdn London Gazette 12/1/1945
P/O W.G. Evans	617 Sqdn London Gazette 12/12/1944
F/Lt A.G. Farthing	617 Sqdn London Gazette 17/7/1945

A/W/C J.E. Fauquier	405 Sqdn London Gazette 4/8/1942
P/O G.E. Fawke	49 Sqdn London Gazette 20/11/1942
P/O A.W. Fearn	57 Sqdn London Gazette 21/4/1944
P/O F.W. Garnet	78 Sqdn London Gazette 19/9/1944
F/Lt E.V. Gavin	617 Sqdn London Gazette 21/9/1945
F/O K. Gill	9 Sqdn London Gazette 11/2/1944
F/O J. Gingles	617 Sqdn London Gazette 8/12/1944
W/O J.I. Gordon	467 Sqdn London Gazette 10/12/1943
F/Lt W.H. Gordon	189 Sqdn London Gazette 22/5/1945
F/O J.M. Grant	49 Sqdn London Gazette 18/8/1943
F/O J.R. Gurney	617 Sqdn London Gazette 13/10/1944
F/LT L.G.A. Hadland	9 Sqdn London Gazette 2/6/1944|
F/O J.L. Hager	617 Sqdn London Gazette 16/2/1945
W/O D. Hamilton	617 Sqdn London Gazette 20/7/1945
F/LT M.L. Hamilton	617 Sqdn London Gazette 16/2/1945
F/O G.J. Harden	106 Sqdn London Gazette 10/9/1943
W/O L.J. Hazell	617 Sqdn London Gazette 12/1/1945
F/O A. Hill	617 Sqdn London Gazette 30/6/1944
W/O G.W. Holden, DFC	25 Sqdn London Gazette 2/9/1941
P/O R.M. Horsley	50 Sqdn London Gazette 6/10/1942
F/O C.H. Houseman	617 Sqdn London Gazette 25/9/1945
W/O J.W. Hutton	617 Sqdn London Gazette 19/9/1944
A/S/L T.C. Iveson	617 Sqdn London Gazette 16/3/1945
W/O A. Jackson	617 Sqdn London Gazette 29/9/1945
F/LT K.S. Jewell	617 Sqdn London Gazette 16/2/1945
P/O J.I.Johnstone	619 Sqdn London Gazette 27/6/1944
A/F/LT R.S.D. Kearns	156 Sqdn London Gazette 10/4/1943
F/O A.E. Kell	463 Sqdn London Gazette 23/5/1944
F/O P. Kelly	49 Sqdn London Gazette 12/8/1943
P/O B.F. Kent	467 Sqdn London Gazette 19/1/1944
P/O L.W.J. King	57 Sqdn London Gazette 22/10/1943
F/O R.E. Knights	619 Sqdn London Gazette 21/4/1944
1st/Lt H.C. Knilans (USA)	617 Sqdn Approved 9/3/1945
P/O G.W. Lancey	97 Sqdn London Gazette 19/6/1943
F/O W.R. Lee	106 Sqdn London Gazette 6/6/1944
P/O N.H. Lloyd	44 Sqdn London Gazette 17/10/1944
F/O D. Luker	617 Sqdn London Gazette 30/7/1944 (Dated 25/1/1946)
W/O M.L. McKay	617 Sqdn London Gazette 20/7/1945
W/O T.J. McLean	617 Sqdn London Gazette 12/12/1944
F/O P.H. Martin	617 Sqdn London Gazette 5/12/1944
F/O K.C. Morieson	617 Sqdn London Gazette 25/5/1945
A/S/L E.P.G. Moyna	617 Sqdn London Gazette 21/4/1944
A/F/LT D.J. Oram	617 Sqdn London Gazette 13/10/1944
W/O W.H. Pengelly	617 Sqdn London Gazette 25/5/1945
A/F/Lt R.H. Petch	76 Sqdn London Gazette 20/4/1943
F/Lt T.H.J. Playford	617 Sqdn London Gazette 12/1/1945
P/O A.R. Poole	97 Sqdn London Gazette 26/3/1943
F/Lt A.F. Poore	106 Sqdn London Gazette 2/6/1944
F/Lt J.L. Powell	617 Sqdn London Gazette 19/3/1946

F/O H.J. Pringle	617 Sqdn London Gazette 15/9/1943
F/O L.T. Pritchard	50 Sqdn London Gazette 15/2/1944
A/F/Lt H.J. Pryor	207 Sqdn London Gazette 23/5/1944
P/O D.A. Rawes	61 Sqdn London Gazette 13/7/43
F/O H.B. Rhude	617 Sqdn London Gazette 13/10/1944
F/Lt C.G. Rogers	617 Sqdn London Gazette 13/4/1945
P/O L.G. Rolton	61 Sqdn London Gazette 2/6/1944
P/O J.K. Roland	617 Sqdn London Gazette 20/7/1945
F/O N.R. Ross	103 Sqdn London Gazette 13/7/1943
F/O F.G. Rumbles	97 Sqdn London Gazette 15/6/1943
W/O A. Rushton	617 Sqdn London Gazette 19/9/1944
P/O J.A. Sanders	49 Sqdn London Gazette 25/4/1944
A/F/Lt K.J. Ryall	617 Sqdn London Gazette 23/3/1945
A/F/Lt J.L. Sayers	467 Sqdn London Gazette 14/11/1944
P/O J. Scannell	405 Sqdn London Gazette 19/1/1945
F/O R.F. Scott-Kiddie	162 Sqdn London Gazette 9/3/1943
P/O D.C. Shea	61 Sqdn London Gazette 19/10/1943
F/O J. Slater	44 Sqdn London Gazette 20/2/1945
W/O R. Smith	617 Sqdn London Gazette 10/9/1944
F/O R.M. Stanford	467 Sqdn London Gazette 23/5/1944
A/F/Lt T.S. Stewart	61 Sqdn London Gazette 24/8/1943
F/O J.K. Stott	617 Sqdn London Gazette 13/10/1944
F/O G.S. Stout	617 Sqdn London Gazette 21/7/1944
A/S/L W.R. Suggitt	428 Sqdn London Gazette 9/7/1943
A/S/L J.B. Tait	51 Sqdn London Gazette 22/10/1940
F/O E. Twells	617 Sqdn London Gazette 13/10/1944
F/O H.W. Cornish-Underwood	617 Sqdn London Gazette 13/11/1944
W/O D.H. Vaughan	617 Sqdn London Gazette 25/5/1945
F/O A.J. Walker	617 Sqdn London Gazette 12/1/1945
F/O J.C. Warburton	57 Sqdn London Gazette 16/2/1945
A/F/Lt A.J. Ward	617 Sqdn London Gazette 13/4/1945
F/O D.T. Watkins	50 Sqdn London Gazette 19/9/1944
F/O J.S. Watson	617 Sqdn London Gazette 30/6/1944
F/O F.H.A. Watts	617 Sqdn London Gazette 27/3/1945
P/O F.W. Weaver	467 Sqdn London Gazette 19/1/1945
F/O R.H. Williams	57 Sqdn London Gazette 14/9/1943
P/O J.E.R. Williams	61 Sqdn London Gazette 2/6/1944
F/O F.E. Willsher	617 Sqdn London Gazette 30/6/1944
F/Lt.D.J. B. Wilson	196 Sqdn London Gazette 14/5/1943
F/O G.A.A. Witherick	617 Sqdn London Gazette 20/2/1945
F/O R.E. Woods	617 Sqdn London Gazette 17/10/1944
A/F/Lt D.R.C. Wyness	50 Sqdn London Gazette 20/4/1943
A/F/Lt E.E.G. Youseman	214 Sqdn London Gazette 12/3/1943

Bar to Distinguished Flying Cross

A/F/Lt S.A. Anning	617 Sqdn London Gazette 4/12/1945
A/F/Lt C.K. Astbury	617 Sqdn London Gazette 28/4/1944
F/Lt J.F. Brookes	617 Sqdn London Gazette 4/12/1945
F/O J. Castagnola	617 Sqdn London Gazette 16/3/1945
F/Lt E.B. Chandler	617 Sqdn London Gazette 13/10/1944
A/S/L J.V. Cockshott	617 Sqdn London Gazette 22/5/1945

F/O L.W. Curtis	617 Sqdn London Gazette 11/4/1944
F/Lt B.J. Dobson	617 Sqdn London Gazette 16/2/1945
S/L G.B. Ellwood	617 Sqdn London Gazette 4/12/1945
A/W/C G.W. Holden	102 Sqdn London Gazette 12/2/1943
F/O A.E. Kell	617 Sqdn London Gazette 6/2/1945
F/O P. Kelly	617 Sqdn London Gazette 9/6/1944
F/O P.H. Martin	617 Sqdn London Gazette 8/5/1945
A/F/Lt D.J. Oram	617 Sqdn London Gazette 22/5/1945
A/S/L F.G. Rumbles	617 Sqdn London Gazette 13/10/1944
F/O J.A. Sanders	617 Sqdn London Gazette 5/12/1944
F/Lt J.L. Sayers	617 Sqdn London Gazette 4/12/1945
W/C J.B. Tait	617 Sqdn London Gazette 5/12/1944
F/Lt D.J.B. Wilson	617 Sqdn London Gazette 28/9/1942

Conspicuous Gallantry Medal

W/O W.G. Bickley	617 Sqdn London Gazette 26/5/1944
W/O B.W. Clayton	51 Sqdn London Gazette 11/6/1943
W/O E. Gosling	617 Sqdn London Gazette 21/9/1945

Distinguished Flying Medal

Sgt S.R. Anderson	467 Sqdn London Gazette 14/9/1943
F/Sgt D.W. Bale	97 Sqdn London Gazette 11/8/1942
F/Sgt W.J.M.L. Barclay	156 Sqdn London Gazette 12/3/1943
Sgt T. Bennett	49 Sqdn London Gazette 9/2/1943
F/Sgt J. Blagborough	617 Sqdn London Gazette 21/9/1945
F/Sgt G.R. Bradbury	617 Sqdn London Gazette 17/7/1945
Sgt R.A. Briars	49 Sqdn London Gazette 9/5/1944
F/Sgt T.S. Cook	61 Sqdn London Gazette 14/5/1943
F/Sgt J.A. Dadge	617 Sqdn London Gazette 17/7/1945
F/Sgt J.M. Dempster	57 Sqdn London Gazette 16/2/1943
F/Sgt P.W. Derham	617 Sqdn London Gazette 13/10/1944
F/Sgt M.G.F. Dowman	617 Sqdn London Gazette 23/5/1944
F/Sgt S.J. Eldridge	50 Sqdn London Gazette 7/12/1943
F/Sgt M. Ellwood	97 Sqdn London Gazette 29/12/1942
Sgt H.W. Felton	50 Sqdn London Gazette 10/12/1943
F/Sgt R. Florence	214 Sqdn London Gazette 16/2/1943
F/Sgt J. Gingles	432 Sqdn London Gazette 10/9/1943
F/Sgt W.C. Grimes	218 Sqdn London Gazette 12/1/1943
Sgt T.H. Goacher	97 Sqdn London Gazette 28/4/1942
Sgt B.A. Gumbley	49 Sqdn London Gazette 18/5/1943
F/Sgt R.L. Hayter	50 Sqdn London Gazette 12/11/1943
F/Sgt R.P. Haywood	617 Sqdn London Gazette 22/5/1945
F/Sgt S.J. Henderson	617 Sqdn London Gazette 17/7/1945
F/Sgt G. Hoyland	106 Sqdn London Gazette 15/8/1944
F/Sgt W. Hume	617 Sqdn London Gazette 15/9/1944
F/Sgt H. Johnson	57 Sqdn London Gazette 23/5/1944
Sgt R.S.D. Kearns	75 Sqdn London Gazette 27/10/1942
F/Sgt A.M. Laughland	214 Sqdn London Gazette 11/6/1943
F/Sgt R.A. Learmouth	619 Sqdn London Gazette 17/12/1943
Sgt J.C.A. Lepine	150 Sqdn London Gazette 27/4/1943
Sgt R. Lucan	207 Sqdn London Gazette 4/9/1943

F/Sgt A.M. McKie	106 Sqdn London Gazette 15/8/1944
Sgt T.J. McLean	102 Sqdn London Gazette 5/1/1943
F/Sgt L. McLellan	617 Sqdn London Gazette 30/6/1944
Sgt R. Machin	49 Sqdn London Gazette 9/5/1944
F/Sgt I.M. Marshall	9 Sqdn London Gazette 11/6/1943
Sgt T.A. Meikle	138 Sqdn London Gazette 29/12/1942
F/Sgt T.G. Muhl	207 Sqdn London Gazette 17/8/1943
F/Sgt D.P. Pearson	50 Sqdn London Gazette 13/12/1944
Sgt G.A. Phillips	50 Sqdn London Gazette 15/6/1943
F/Sgt R.V. Pooley	50 Sqdn London Gazette 11/2/1944
F/Sgt G.R. Price	106 Sqdn London Gazette 14/5/1943
Sgt A.E. Quinton	50 Sqdn London Gazette 24/10/1941
Sgt E.A. Roberts	61 Sqdn London Gazette 18/5/1943
F/Sgt R.E. Salter	617 Sqdn London Gazette 25/5/1945
F/S J.B. Scannell	35 Sqdn London Gazette 14/5/1943
F/Sgt J.K. Stott	61 Sqdn London Gazette 20/4/1943
F/Sgt K.L. Sumner	44 Sqdn London Gazette 26/5/1944
F/Sgt F.C. Temple	617 Sqdn London Gazette 12/11/1943
F/Sgt T.J. Trebilcock	617 Sqdn London Gazette 25/9/1945
Sgt A. Ward	49 Sqdn London Gazette 9/5/1944
F/Sgt P.L. Whittaker	617 Sqdn London Gazette 7/12/1945
Sgt S.J. Whittingham	214 Sqdn London Gazette 14/5/1943
F/Sgt G.A. Witherick	405 Sqdn London Gazette 20/12/1942

Bar to Distinguished Flying Medal

F/Sgt T.H. Goacher	619 Sqdn London Gazette 13/8/1943

Air Force Cross

A/S/L J.F. Brookes	22 OTU Operational Command! London Gazette 1/1/1945

Mention in Dispatches

F/O E.A. Barnett	49 Sqdn London Gazette 8/6/1944
P/O G.L. Cheshire	102 Sqdn London Gazette 17/3/1941
Sgt H.G. Clarke	617 Sqdn London Gazette 8/6/1944
F/Sgt W.T. Eaves	617 Sqdn London Gazette 1/1/1945
F/Sgt M. Ellwood	5 Group London Gazette 1/1/1943
F/O C.E.M. Graham	5 Group London Gazette 8/6/1944
Sgt W. Johnson	617 Sqdn London Gazette 8/6/1944
P/O L.W.J. King	57 Sqdn London Gazette 2/6/1943
S/L J.B. Tait	35 Sqdn London Gazette 24/9/1941

Foreign Awards

Croix de Guerre (Belgium)

F/Sgt L.C. Doyle	617 Sqdn London Gazette 27/6/1943
	(With Palm)

Order of Leopold (Belgium)

F/Lt F.J. Corringe   617 Sqdn London Gazette 27/6/1947
                                                          (With Palm)

Legion of Honour (France)

G/Cpt J.E. Fauquier   617 Sqdn London Gazette

Croix de Guerre (France)

C/Cpt J.E. Fauquier   617 Sqdn London Gazette
                                                          (With Palm)
F/O K. Gill   617 Sqdn London Gazette 5/6/1946
                                                  (With Silver Star)

Medal of Valour (Russia)

A/F/Lt E.B. Chandler   617 Sqdn London Gazette 11/4/1944

Distinguished Flying Cross (United States of America)

A/W/C C.C. Calder   617 Sqdn London Gazette 15/5/1945
1st Lt H.C. Knilans (USAF)   617 Sqdn London Gazette 9/3/1945

Appendix V

617 Squadron Aircraft

Lancasters

DV 155		To 617 Squadron 31/5/1943. To 44 Squadron June 1943. Lost 3/4 September 1943.
DV 156		To 617 Squadron May 1943. To 50 Squadron July 1943. Lost 12/13 July 1943 Turin.
DV 344	Letter M	To A.V. Roe 13/10/1943. To 106 Squadron 22/10/1943. To 61 Squadron 17/11/1943. Missing 2/1/1944.
DV 246		To 617 Squadron August 1943. To 1661/54/5 MU's. Scrapped August 1947.
DV 380		To 617 Squadron November 1943. Scrapped March 1946.
DV 382	Letter G	To 617 Squadron (Squadron Leader Suggitt) 11/11/1943. Flew into a hill in Sussex 13/2/1944, time 0830.
DV 385	Letter A	To 617 Squadron 11/11/1943. Scrapped 9/11/1946.
DV 391	Letter W	To 617 Squadron November 1943. Scrapped October 1946.
DV 392	Letter T	To 625 Squadron 23/11/1943. Missing on trip to Berlin 4/12/1943.
DV 394	Letter M	To 617 Squadron (Flight Lieutenant Cooper) 25/11/1943. Missing on trip to Munich 25/4/1944.
DV 398	Letter Z	To 617 Squadron (Flight Lieutenant Rice) 30/11(1943. Crashed at Merbes-le-Chateau Belgium 21/12/1943.
DV 402	Letter X	To 617 Squadron December 1943. Scrapped November 1945.
DV 403	Letter G	To 617 Squadron (Flight Lieutenant Edward) 10/12/1943. Lost on a trip to Wizernes 25/6/1944.
DV 993	Letter T	To 617 Squadron 23/11/1943. Scrapped 24/1/1944.

DV 393	Letter T	To 617 Squadron November 1943. To 9 Squadron March 1945. To 38 MUFebruary 1946. Scrapped May 1947.
ED 735	Letter R	To 617 Squadron (Flight Lieutenant Youseman) 27/3/1943. Missing at sea 19/11/1943.
ED 842	Letter O	To 617 Squadron April 1944.
ED 763	Letter D or R	To 617 Squadron April 1943. Scrapped 14/5/1945.
ED 765	Letter M	To 617 Squadron (Flight Lieutenant Kellaway) 8/7/1943. Burnt at Ashley Walk 6/8/1943.
ED 817	Letter X	To 617 Squadron (Prototype). Scrapped January 1945.
ED 825	Letter E	To 617 Squadron (Flying Officer Weedon) June 1943. Lost at Doullens France 10/12/1943.
ED 886	Letter O	To 617 Squadron (Warrant Officer Bull) 23/4/1943). Lost on trip to Doullens France 11/12/1943; hit a tree on 19/10/1943, pilot looking at bomb aimer's map at the time.
ED 906	Letter J	To 617 Squadron 23/4/1943. Scrapped 29/7/1947.
ED 909	Letter P	To 617 Squadron 23/4/1943. Damaged on the Dams Raid. Returned to 617 Squadron 12/6/1943 Hit a tree 30/10/1943 in poor visibility. Scrapped. 29/7/1947.
ED 912	Letter N	To 617 Squadron 3/5/1943. Scrapped 26/9/1946.
ED 915	Letter Q	To 617 Squadron 28/4/1943. Scrapped 8/10/1946.
ED 918	Letter F	To 617 Squadron (Flight Lieutenant O'Shaughnessy) 30/4/1943. Damaged 17/5/1943 on Dams Raid, returned to Squadron 29/5/1943. Burnt in crash 21/1/1944 Snettisham Norfolk.
ED 921	Letter W	To 617 Squadron 30/4/1943. Damaged 17/5/1943 on Dams Raid. Scrapped 26/5/1945.
ED 923	Letter T	To 617 Squadron 2/5/1943.
ED 924	Letter Y	To 617 Squadron 30/4/1943. Scrapped 23/9/1946.
ED 929	Letter L	To 617 Squadron 30/4/1943. Hit a tree, damaged 7/6/1943. Scrapped 7/10/1946.
ED 932	Letter G	To 617 Squadron 30/4/1943. To 61 Squadron 27/8/1946. Scrapped 29/7/1947.
ED 933		To 617 Squadron 2/5/1943, still with 617 Squadron in 1945. Scrapped 7/10/1946.
ED 936	Letter H	To 617 Squadron 12/5/1943. Damaged on Dams Raid, returned to 617 Squadron 17/7/1943. Crashed at Woodhall Spa 22/7/1943. 65 hours only.
ED 999	Letter A	To 49 Squadron 28/6/1943. To 44 Squadron 24/10/1943. Missing 24/12/1943.
EE 130	Letter S	To 617 Squadron May 1943(Flight Lieutenant Allsebrook). Lost on Dortmund-Ems Canal trip 16/9/1943 at Berge Shovede.
EE 106		To 617 Squadron 20/5/1943. To 619 Squadron, lost in sea 30/9/1943.

EE 131	Letter C	To 617 Squadron 28/8/1943. Crash landed in Russia Molotovsk 11-12/9/1944 (Tirpitz Operation).
EE 144	Letter S	To 617 Squadron (Acting Wing Commander Holden) 3/5/1943. Lost on Dortmund-Ems Canal trip 16/9/1943.
EE 145		To 617 Squadron 31/5/1943. Crashed at Woodhall Spa 7/6/1943. 3 hours 55 minutes only.
EE 148	Letter U	To 617 Squadron 4/6/1943. To 626 Squadron 15/2/1944. Lost on Mailly Raid 3/4/1944.
EE 146	Letter K	To 617 Squadron June 1943. Hit trees near Ganwood Yorks 8/9/1943. Scrapped 24/4/1945.
EE 149		To 617 Squadron 4/6/1943.
EE 150	Letter Z	To 617 Squadron 6/6/1943. To 619 Squadron 3/12/1943. Scrapped 28/12/1943.
JA 894	Letter C	To 49 Squadron July 1943. To 617 Squadron September 1943.
JA 874	Letter E	To 61 Squadron July 1943 (Flying Officer Divall) to 617 Squadron September 1943. Lost on Dortmund Ems Canal trip 16-17/9/1943, at Reike (Flight Lieutenant Wilson). Crashed at Ladbergen Germany 15-16/9/1943.
JA 848	Letter X	
JA 981	Letter N	To 617 Squadron September 1943. Missing in sea 15/9/1943 after recall. 41 hours only.
JA 144	Letter N	To 617 Squadron (Flight Lieutenant Knight) September 1943. Lost on Dortmund Ems Canal trip at Den Ham near Meer, Holland, 16/9/1943. 37 hours only.
JB 139	Letter V	To 49 Squadron (Flying Officer Cheney) 24/8/1943. To 617 Squadron 22/7/1944. Lost at Brest France 5/8/1944.
JB 135	Letter X	To 57 Squadron 23/8/1943. To 630 Squadron 15/11/1943. Missing 24/11/1943.
JB 320	Letter U	To 57 Squadron 19/9/1943. Missing 23/10/1943.
JB 370	Letter U	To 57 Squadron 1/10/1943. Missing 7/7/1944.
EE 197	Letter Y	To 57 Squadron 15/4/1943. Scrapped 28/1/1944.
LM 489	Letter L	From 61 Squadron to 617 Squadron 13/7/1944. Scrapped 15/1/1947.
LM 695	Letter N	To 463 Squadron 12/5/1944. To 617 Squadron 14/8/1944. To 15 Squadron 29/6/1945. To 617 Squadron 4/6/1946. Scrapped 23/3/1947.
LM 482	Letter Q	Lost 7/10/1944, crashed at Markt near Lorrach Baden. (F/Lt Howard)
ME 339		To 617 Squadron 13/3/1945. To 9 Squadron 27/3/1945. Scrapped 22/5/1947.
ME 559	Letter Y	To 617 Squadron December 1943. Crash landed at Kegostrov in Russia 12/9/1944.
ME 555	Letter C	To 617 Squadron 16/12/1943. To 9 Squadron 1945. Scrapped 1947.

ME 557	Letter S	To 617 Squadron (Flight Lieutenant Reid VC) 12/12/1943. Lost on raid to Reilly Montagne France, crashed near Germaine.
ME 560		To 617 Squadron 16/12/1943. Burnt out 15/7/1944.
ME 561	Letter T	To 617 Squadron (Flying Officer Joplin) 20/12/1943. Struck ground in fog 22/12/1943.
ME 543	Letter F	To 429 Squadron 8/3/1945. Scrapped 12/9/1947.
ME 562	Letter Z	To 617 Squadron December 1943. Scrapped January 1947.
LM 492		Damaged in Russia 13/9/1944. Collided with a Mosquito DZ 518 while taxying 25/11/1944. Scrapped 1947.
LM 485	Letter W	From 15 Squadron to 617 Squadron 7/3/1944. Wrecked 6/4/1945 at Brest France.
ND 683	Letter P	To 49 Squadron March 1944. Lost 22/6/1944.
ND 339	Letter Z	To 106 Squadron 12/12/1943. Missing 5/7/1944. Scrapped 8/7/1944.
ND 554	Letter N	To 630 Squadron 27/1/1944. Used by Watts with 617 Squadron but belonging to 630 Squadron. Lost 9/2/1945.
ND 583	Letter P	To 630 Squadron 5/2/1944. Lost 16/3/1944.
NF 920	Letter E	617 Squadron aircraft (Flying Officer Carey). Landed in Sweden after Tirpitz attack 29/10/1944. Crashed near Potjus Sweden.
NF 923	Letter M	To 617 Squadron (Warrant Officer Stout) 13/8/1944. Missing Lochem Holland 24/9/1944.
NG 181	Letter M	To 617 Squadron from 195 Squadron March 1945. Scrapped October 1945.
NG 445	Letter E	From 617 Squadron to 44 Squadron. Scrapped April 1948.
NG 489	Letter M	To 617 Squadron then 44 Squadron. To 15 Squadron 29/5/1945. To 44 Squadron 17/3/1947.
NG 340	Letter L	To 617 Squadron 21/1/1945. To 15 Squadron 29/5/1945. To 44 Squadron 4/7/1946.
NG 228	Letter V	To 617 Squadron (Squadron Leader Powell) 11/12/1944. Missing on attack on Lützow, crashed at Caseburg near Poznam 16-17/4/1945.
NG 494	Letter B	To 617 Squadron 17/1/1945. To 15 Squadron 29/5/1945. To 44 Squadron 4/7/1946.
NG 496	Letter B	To 433 Squadron February 1945. Scrapped 30/11/1946.
NG 180		To 617 Squadron (Squadron Leader Wyness) 27/9/1944. Crashed at Bellingen Germany 7/10/1944.
NG 339		To 617 Squadron 17/1/1945. To 15 Squadron 29/5/1945. To 44 Squadron 16/8/1946. Scrapped 16/10/1947.
PB 416	Letter V	To 617 Squadron (Flying Officer Levy) August

		1944. Crashed at Rukkedalen Norway 17/9/1944.
PB 996	Letter C	To 617 Squadron 20/2/1945. Scrapped 18/11/1947.
PB 415	Letter O	To 617 Squadron August 1944. Scrapped 18/4/1945.
ND 631	Letter Z or B	To 44 Squadron 20/2/1944, Missing 10-. 11/4/1945.
PD 238	Letter H	To 617 Squadron July 1944. Wrecked 7/11/1945.
PD 233	Letter G	To 617 Squadron (Flight Lieutenant Pryor) 29/7/1944. Lost Bergen Norway 12/1/1945.
PD 371	Letter S	617 aircraft. Scrapped May 1947. To 617 Squadron 3/3/1945. To 156 Squadron 8/4/1945. To 15 Squadron 4/6/1945. Scrapped 30/9/1950.
PD 114	Letter B	To 617 Squadron 1/3/1945. Scrapped May 1947.
PD 121	Letter Z	To 617 Squadron 12/3/1945. To 15 Squadron 4/6/1945. Scrapped 19/5/1947.
PD 772	Letter L	To 617 Squadron March 1945.
PB 998	Letter N	To 617 Squadron 24/2/1945. Scrapped 18/11/1947.
PD 131	Letter A	To 617 Squadron 11/3/1945. To 15 Squadron 4/6/1945. Scrapped May 19 1947.
PD 116	Letter W	To 617 Squadron 1/3/1945. Scrapped 11/3/1948.
PD 130	Letter D	To 617 Squadron 6/3/1945. Scrapped March 11 1948.
PD 118	Letter B	To 617 Squadron March 3 1945. Scrapped may 22 1947.
PD 129		To 617 Squadron 3/3/1945. Scrapped 2/6/1947.
PD 132	Letter E	To 617 Squadron March 1945. Scrapped March 1948.
PD 115	Letter C	To 617 Squadron 1/3/1945. Scrapped May 1947.
PD 112	Letter Z	To 617 Squadron 26/2/1945. Dropped first Grand Slam Bomb 14 March 1945. Scrapped 4/8/1945.
PD 134	Letter Y	To 617 Squadron 11/3/1945. Scrapped November 1947.
PB 735	Letter W	To 625 Squadron October 1944. To 617 Squadron March 1945. Scrapped May 1947.
PD 128	Letter N	To 617 Squadron 6/3/1945. To 15 Squadron 4/6/1945. Scrapped 25/3/1948.
PD 117	Letter X	To 617 Squadron (Flight Lieutenant Gumbley) 1/3/1945. Missing 21/3/1945.
PB 596	Letter C	To 617 Squadron March 1945. Crashed September 1947.
PD 133	Letter P	To 61 Squadron 13/3/1945. Scrapped 22/5/1947.
PB 998	Letter D	To 617 Squadron 24/2/1945. Scrapped 18/11/1947.
PD 113	Letter T	To 617 Squadron 26/2/1945. Scrapped 6/11/1947.
PD 135	Letter W	To 617 Squadron March 1945. Scrapped March 1948.
PD 136		To 617 Squadron 27/4/1945. Scrapped 14/3/1947.

PD 139			To 617 Squadron (Pilot Lt W.E. Adams USA) 25/3/1945. Crashed Brunswick 16/7/1945, made a forced landing.
PD 371			To 617 Squadron 6/2/1945. Scrapped 22/5/1946.
PD 181	Letter Z		To 617 Squadron 3/3/1945. Scrapped 22/5/1947.
W 4949			617 Squadron and 619 Squadron. Crashed 5/9/1943

Mosquitos

Mosquito 16	ML 976	Letter N	To 109 Squadron 27/3/1944.
Mosquito 7	MS 993	Letter N	To 617 Squadron 11/4/1944. To 514 Squadron 14/4/1944. Lost 13/9/1944, crashed landed in Switzerland.
Mosquito 4	DZ 421	Letter C	
Mosquito 6	NS 953	Letter N	To 515 Squadron 19/3/1944. Missing 29/10/1944.
Mosquito	NS 955	Letter N	To 515 Squadron 23/3/1944.
Mosquito	ML 935	Letter M	105, 692, 627 and 109 Squadrons.
Mosquito 4	DZ 637	Letter O	627, 692 Squadrons. Missing 12/7/1944.
Mosquito 4	DZ 547	Letter E	627 Squadron 25/3/1944. Scrapped 11/10/1946.
Mosquito 6	DZ 525	Letter S	617 Squadron May 1944.
Mosquito	DZ 641	Letter C	692 Squadron 6/4/1944. To 627 Squadron 8/4/1945. To 109 Squadron 1/10/1945.
Mosquito	NT 202	Letter N	To 617 Squadron 5/5/1944. (F/O Duffy). Crashed Wainfleet Bombing Range 7/8/1944 total wreck.
Mosquito 20	KB 215	Letter N	Scottish AV 24/4/1944. To 139 Squadron 11/7/1944. To 627 Squadron 24/7/1944.
Mosquito 16	ML 976		109 Squadron 27/3/1944. Scrapped 21/9/1944.
Mosquito	NT 205	Letter L	617 Squadron 5/5/1944 left 617 3/9/1946.

Mustang

Mustang	HB 937	Letter N	Sailed on S.S. Brady to UK 18/5/1944. To 617 Squadron 25/6/1944. To 541 Squadron 14/5/1945. Scrapped 14/3/1947.

Some aircraft listed here are not recorded as being on 617 Squadron's strength but are shown to have flown on operations with the Squadron; it appears borrowing of aircraft was a common occurrence, especially the Mosquito.

Appendix VI

617 Squadron Achievements

First operation 16 May 1943: Dams Raid.
Last operation 25 April 1945: Hitler's Eagle's Nest, Berchtesgaden.
Number of operations: 95
Casualties: 187
Awards:

    Victoria Cross: 2.
    DSO: 13.
    Bar to DSO: 5.
    DFC: 68
    Bar to DFC: 23
    CGM: 4
    DFM: 25.
    Bar to DFM: 1.
    Foreign Awards: 9.
    MID: 3
    Total Awards to 617 Squadron   153

Targets:

    Dams.
    Canals.
    Factories.
    Rocket Sites.
    U Boat Pens.
    Capital German Ships.
    Viaducts.
    Aircraft lost 32.
    Aircraft used on operations 154.

Appendix VII

Wing Commander G.P. Gibson	24.3.43
Squadron Leader G.W. Holden	3.8.43
Squadron Leader H.B. Martin (Temporary)	16.9.43
Wind Commander G.L. Cheshire	10.11.43
Wing Commander J.B. Tait	12.7.44
Group Captain J.E. Fauquier	29.12.44
Wing Commander J.E. Grindon	28.4.45
Wing Commander C. Fothergill	9.8.45
Squadron Leader C.K. Saxelby	4.46
Wing Commander C.D. Milne	21.4.47

(Appointed to Command Squadron for the period of its Good Will visit to the United States. Squadron Leader Saxelby resumed command afterwards).

Squadron Leader P.G. Brodie	24.2.48
Squadron Leader W.H. Thallon	3.5.50
Squadron Leader M.J. O'Bryen-Nichols	13.6.52
Squadron Leader D. Roberts	22.12.52
Squadron Leader J.A. Ruck	15.4.54

(Squadron disbanded on 15 December 1955).

Wing Commander D. Bower	1.5.58
Wing Commander L.G.A. Bastard (AFC)	7.5.60
Wing Commander H.G. Currell MVO, DFC, AFC	9.11.62
Wing Commander D.G.,L. Heywood	22.3.65
Wing Commander R.C. Allen	23.3.67
Wing Commander C.A. Vasey	14.3.69
Wing Commander F.M.A. Hines	29.3.71
Wing Commander V.L. Warrington	22.10.73
Wing Commander R.B. Gilvary	8.9.75
Squadron Leader J.N. Stephenson-Oliver (later Wing Commander)	5.77
Squadron Leader J.K. Walters	5.79
Wing Commander J.N. Herbertson	7.79

(Squadron disbanded on 31 December 1981).

Wing Commander A.P. Harrison	1.1.1983

Other titles from Goodalls

WING LEADER
The thrilling story of the top-scoring Allied fighter pilot of World War II – Air Vice-Marshal 'Johnnie' Johnson CB CBE DSO and 2 Bars, DFC and Bar. 'Johnnie' shot down no fewer than 38 enemy aircraft.
£3.50   ISBN 0 907579 13 2

LANCASTER TARGET
The story of a RAF Bomber Command crew's tour of operations over Germany, told by S/Ldr. Jack Currie, DFC, was featured in the BBC TV documentary 'The Lancaster Legend'.
£3.50   ISBN 0 907579 00 0

LANCASTER TO BERLIN
This book by Canadian Pathfinder pilot, Walter Thompson, DFC and Bar concentrates on Bomber Command's 1943–44 offensive against the 'Big City'.
£3.50   ISBN 0 907579 04 3

REAR GUNNER PATHFINDERS
Ron Smith DFM writes a vivid, action-packed story of 65 operations in the rear turret of a Lancaster, mainly with 156 Squadron of the Pathfinder Force.
£3.50   ISBN 0 907579 02 7

ONLY OWLS AND BLOODY FOOLS FLY AT NIGHT
Group Captain Tom Sawyer DFC records five and a half wartime years with RAF Bomber Command.
£3.50   ISBN 0 907579 07 8

MOSQUITO VICTORY
This sequel to S/Ldr. Jack Currie's LANCASTER TARGET describes the life of a bomber pilot on 'rest' at an O.T.U. Plus Mosquito operations.
£3.50   ISBN 0 907579 03 5

NO MOON TONIGHT
One of the greatest books ever written about Bomber Command – a classic of its kind – by Don Charlwood, a wartime navigator with the RAAF.

£2.95   ISBN 0 907579 06 X

ENEMY COAST AHEAD
Wing Commander Guy Gibson VC contributes what is widely regarded as one of the most brilliant and accurate descriptions of the raid by Lancasters of 617 Squadron – the Dambusters – on the Moehne and Eder Dams.

£2.95   ISBN 0 907579 08 6

THE AUGSBURG RAID
This raid was one of RAF Bomber Command's most daring attacks of World War II. Twelve Lancasters from Nos. 44 & 97 Squadrons flew the 500 miles to Augsburg in broad daylight at 100 ft.

£7.95 (hardback)   ISBN 0 907579 09 4

A WAAF IN BOMBER COMMAND
'Pip' Beck's sensitively-written true story of a RAF Bomber Command wartime R/T operator.

£3.25   ISBN 0 907579 12 4

WINGS OVER GEORGIA
S/Ldr. Jack Currie DFC tells the story of his initial flying training with the US Army Air Corps under the Arnold Scheme.

£2.95   ISBN 0 907579 11 6

PATHFINDER
Air Vice-Marshall Donald Bennett's epic account of the creation under his command of the mighty Pathfinder Force of Bomber Command.

£2.95   ISBN 0 907579 05 1

BOMBER PILOT
Written by Group Captain Leonard Cheshire when he was on No. 35 Squadron of Bomber Command. A classic.

£2.95   ISBN 0 907579 10 8